WHO *IS* JESUS?

The Crucial Questions Series
By R. C. Sproul

WHO *Is* JESUS?

CAN I TRUST *the* BIBLE?

DOES *Prayer* CHANGE THINGS?

CAN I *Know* GOD'S WILL?

HOW SHOULD *I Live* IN THIS WORLD?

CRUCIAL
QUESTIONS
No. 1

WHO *IS* JESUS?

R.C. SPROUL

ℝ

Reformation Trust

PUBLISHING

A DIVISION OF LIGONIER MINISTRIES · ORLANDO, FLORIDA

Who Is Jesus?

© 1983, 1999, 2009 by R. C. Sproul

Previously published as *Who Is Jesus?* (1983) and as part of *Following Christ* (1991) by Tyndale House Publishers, and as *Who Is Jesus?* by Ligonier Ministries (1999).

Published by Reformation Trust
a division of Ligonier Ministries
400 Technology Park, Lake Mary, FL 32746
www.Ligonier.org   www.ReformationTrust.com

Printed in the United States of America

Cover design: Gearbox Studios
Interior design and typeset: Katherine Lloyd, The DESK, Colorado Springs

Unless otherwise noted, Scripture quotations are from The Holy Bible, English Standard Version®, copyright © 2001 by Crossway Bibles, a publishing ministry of Good News Publishers. Used by permission. All rights reserved.

Scripture quotations marked NIV are from the HOLY BIBLE, NEW INTERNATIONAL VERSION®. NIV®. Copyright © 1973, 1978, 1984 by International Bible Society. Used by permission of Zondervan. All rights reserved.

Scripture quotations marked KJV are from The Holy Bible, King James Version.

Library of Congress Cataloging-in-Publication Data

Sproul, R. C. (Robert Charles), 1939-
 Who is Jesus? / R.C. Sproul.
  p. cm. -- (The crucial questions series)
 First published as: Who Is Jesus? 1983. Following Christ. Wheaton, Ill. : Tyndale House Publishers, 1991. Who Is Jesus? Ligonier Ministries, 1999.
 ISBN 978-1-56769-181-8
 1. Jesus Christ--Person and offices. I. Sproul, R. C. (Robert Charles), 1939- Following Christ. II. Title.
 BT203.S67 2009
 232--dc22

2009018825

Contents

WILL THE REAL JESUS
PLEASE STAND UP?

There are vast numbers of portraits of Jesus in the art galleries of this world. These images are often so conflicting that they offer little help in achieving an accurate picture of what Christ looked like during the period of His incarnation. This multiplicity of images parallels the widespread confusion about Jesus' identity that exists in the world today.

We need Christ—the *real* Christ. A Christ born of empty speculation or created to squeeze into the philosopher's pattern simply won't do. A recycled Christ, a Christ of compromise, can redeem no one. A Christ watered down, stripped of power, debased of glory, reduced to a symbol, or made impotent by scholarly surgery is not Christ but Antichrist.

The prefix *anti* can mean "against" or "instead of." In language, there is a difference, but in life, it is a distinction without a difference, because to supplant the real Jesus with a substitute is to work against Christ. To change or distort the real Christ is to oppose Him with a false Christ.

No person in history has provoked as much study, criticism, prejudice, or devotion as Jesus of Nazareth. The titanic influence of this man makes Him a chief target of the arrows of criticism and a prime object of revision according to the interpreter's prejudice. Thus, the portrait of the historical Jesus has been altered to suit the fancies of those seeking to line Him up on their side, to make of Him an ally in a host of militant causes, many of which are mutually exclusive. In the theologian's laboratory, Jesus is treated like a chameleon; He is forced to adapt to the backdrop painted by the theologian.

Rigorous academic attempts have been made to get behind the New Testament portrait of Jesus, to discover the "real" historical Jesus. These attempts to penetrate the wall of history, to peek behind the veil of the so-called primitive

apostolic witness, have taught us much about the prejudice of the scholars but have added little or nothing to our
understanding of the real Jesus. What the scholars discovered behind the veil was a Jesus created in their own images
according to their own prejudices. The nineteenth-century
liberals found a "liberal" Jesus; the existentialists found an
existential hero; and the Marxists discovered a political revolutionary. Idealists found an idealistic Jesus and pragmatists
discovered a pragmatic Christ. To search behind or beyond
the New Testament is to go on a snipe hunt equipped with
the flashlights of pride and prejudice.

Then there is the scissors-and-paste Jesus. He is fash-
ioned by those who seek within the Bible a core or kernel of
tradition about Christ that is authentic. The things they see
as unnecessary extras, the accretions of myth and legend,
are excised by the scissors to expose the real Jesus. It seems
so scientific, but it is all done with mirrors. The magician's
art leaves us with the portrait of Rudolf Bultmann or John
A. T. Robinson, and again the real Jesus is obscured. By
preserving a modicum of New Testament data, we think
we have avoided subjectivity. However, the result is the
same—a Jesus shaped by the bias of the scholar wielding
the scissors and getting his hands sticky from the paste.

The story is told of the vagrant who knocked at the

farmer's door and politely inquired about employment as a handyman. The farmer cautiously put the man to work on a trial basis to measure his skill. The first task was to split logs for firewood, which the stranger finished in record time. The next task was to plow the fields, which he did in just a few hours. The farmer was pleasantly astonished; it seemed he had stumbled on a modern-day Hercules. The third task was less laborious. Taking the hired man to the barn, the farmer pointed to a large pile of potatoes and instructed him to sort them into two piles: those that were of prime quality were to be put in one receptacle and those of inferior grade in another. The farmer was curious when his miracle-working laborer failed to report in as rapidly as he had with the other tasks. After several hours, the farmer went to the barn to investigate. No perceptible change was evident in the pile of potatoes. One receptacle contained three potatoes and the other had only two. "What's wrong?" demanded the farmer. "Why are you moving so slowly?" A look of defeat was written on the hired man's face as he threw up his hands and replied, "It's the decisions in life that are difficult."

The scissors-and-paste method suffers from the problem of determining in advance what is authentic and what is myth in the biblical portrait of Jesus. What Bultmann discards into the basket of husks, another scholar puts into the basket of kernels. What Bultmann calls prime, another discards as inferior.

Evidence Is Compelling

The problem is simple. It lies not with the "shoddy" reporting of the New Testament authors or the "sloppy" documents of history we call the Gospels. It was Emil Brunner, the Swiss theologian, who blew the whistle on nineteenth-century liberalism. Brunner's verdict was as simple as it was inflammatory. The problem, he said, is unbelief.

Brunner was not speaking about unbelief based on insufficient evidence. To withhold belief because the evidence doesn't support the claims is an honorable and wise response. Likewise, to believe against poor evidence is credulity, the mark of the fool, and brings no honor to God.

However, the evidence about Jesus is compelling, so withholding belief in Him is to commit an immoral act. Unbelief is judged by Jesus not as an intellectual error but as a hostile act of prejudice against God Himself. This sort of unbelief is destructive to the church and to the people of God.

How could such blatant unbelief not only attack the Christian church but in several instances capture whole seminaries and even entire denominations? Why don't people who reject the New Testament portrait of Jesus simply abandon Christianity altogether and leave the church to less-educated mortals who need a fanciful Jesus as a religious crutch?

The nineteenth century brought an intellectual and moral crisis to the church—the rise of liberal theology that flatly rejected the supernatural core of the New Testament. This crisis eventually pressed hard on very practical matters. If the leaders of a church or the faculty of a seminary wake up one morning and discover they no longer believe what the Bible teaches or the church confesses, what are their options?

The most obvious option (and the first expected of honorable men) is that they would declare their unbelief and politely leave the church. If they control the power structures of the church, however, they have practical questions to consider. By vocation and training, their jobs are tied to the church. The church represents a multibillion-dollar financial investment, an established cultural institution with millions of active constituent members and a proven effective vehicle for social reform. These factors make declaring unbelief to the world and closing the doors to the churches less attractive. The course of least resistance is to *redefine* Christianity.

Redefining Christianity is no easy task. Christianity has been given definition by two weighty factors: (1) the existence of a body of literature that includes primary sources about the founder and teacher of the Christian faith, Jesus of Nazareth; (2) the existence of two millennia of church tradition, which includes points of disagreement about particular issues of debate among denominations, but which reveals a remarkable unity of confession about the essentials of Christianity. To redefine Christianity requires one to neutralize the authority of the Bible and relativize the authority of the creeds. The struggle of the church for the past 150 years has been precisely at these two points. It is not by accident that the eye of the storm of controversy within the seminaries and the church in our day has focused on issues concerning the Bible and the creeds. Why? Not simply because of words on paper, but because of Christ. One must banish the Christ of the Bible and the Christ of the creeds in order to redefine Christianity.

The church is called "the body of Christ." Some refer to it as "the continuing incarnation." Surely the church exists to embody and carry out the mission of Christ. For this reason, the church is inconceivable without Christ. Yet the church is not Christ. It is founded by Christ, formed by Christ, commissioned by Christ, and endowed by Christ. It is ruled by Christ, sanctified by Christ, and protected by Christ. But it is not Christ. The church can preach salvation and nurture the saved, but it cannot save. The church can preach, exhort, rebuke, and admonish against sin, it can proclaim the forgiveness of sin and it can give theological definition to sin, but the church cannot atone for sin.

Cyprian declared, "He cannot have God for his Father who does not have the church for his Mother." We need the church as urgently as a starving baby needs his mother's milk. We cannot grow or be nourished without the church. Possessing Christ and despising the church is an intolerable contradiction. We cannot have Christ without embracing the church. However, it is possible to have the church without truly embracing Christ. Augustine described the church as a *corpus permixtum*, a "mixed body" of tares and wheat, of unbelievers and believers existing side by side. This means unbelief can gain entrance into the church. But it never can gain entrance into Christ.

The Christ we believe, the Christ we trust, must be true if we are to be redeemed. A false Christ or a substitute Christ cannot redeem. If it is thought unlikely that the biblical Christ can redeem, it is even less likely that the speculative Christ of human invention can redeem. Apart from the Bible, we know nothing of consequence concerning the real Jesus. Ultimately our faith stands or falls with the biblical Jesus. Lay aside theories of biblical inspiration if you must, doing so at your own peril, but even apart from inspiration the New Testament represents the *primary sources*—the earliest documents of those who knew Him, the record of those who studied under Him and were eyewitnesses to His ministry. They are the most objective historical sources we have.

Men Who Wrote with an Agenda

Some demur at this point, calling attention to the obvious fact that the New Testament portrait of Jesus comes to us from the pens of biased men who had an agenda. The Gospels are not history, they say, but redemptive history, with the accent on efforts to persuade men to follow Jesus. Well, certainly the writers had an agenda, but it was not a *hidden* agenda. The apostle John says forthrightly: "These [things] are written so that you may believe that Jesus is the Christ, the Son of God, and that by believing you may have life in his name" (John 20:31).

The fact that the biblical writers were believers and were zealous to persuade others counts for their veracity. Had they been unbelievers while exhorting others to believe, they would have been guilty of duplicity. Of course, men can be mistaken about what they proclaim, but the fact that they believed their own message, even unto death, should enhance rather than weaken their credibility.

Theirs was indeed a record of redemptive history. It was *redemptive* because they were not writing from the standpoint of neutral, disinterested historians. It was *history* because they insisted that their testimony was true.

At this point, a practical question emerges from the streetwise and the hard-nosed skeptic, who seeks to discredit the biblical Christ by exposing the apostolic Christ as a fantasy. They argue that if the closest associates of Jesus were biased (in that they were believers), laborious scholarship to discover the "real" Jesus makes little sense. If all we know about Jesus is learned through the witness of the apostles—if they are the "screen" through which we must gaze to see Him—our efforts seem pointless.

The answer is that the historical Jesus did not live in a vacuum; He is known at least in part by the way He transformed those around Him.

I want to know the Jesus who radicalized Matthew, who transformed Peter, who turned Saul of Tarsus upside down on the Damascus Road. If these firsthand witnesses can't get me to the "real" Jesus, who can? If not through friends and loved ones, how can anyone be known?

If the apostles can't lead me to Jesus, my only options are to scale the fortress of heaven by sheer mystical subjectivism, embracing the oldest of all heresies, Gnosticism, or to pitch my tent with the camp of skeptics who dismiss Jesus from the realm of significant truth altogether. Give me the biblical Christ or give me nothing. Do it quickly, please, as the options give me nothing save the frustration of fruitless laborious research.

Jesus said: "For what does it profit a man to gain the whole world and forfeit his soul? For what can a man give in return for his soul?" (Mark 8:36–37). Jesus put an enormous price tag on the human soul. For that, I am grateful. I like to think my soul has worth, and I would hate to squander it on an empty Christ, a Christ of subjective speculation. However, this is what we are doing when we embrace anything less than a real Christ. We are playing with human souls— the very souls Christ poured out His life to redeem.

Gaining a True Picture of Jesus

There are different methods we could use to arrive at our picture of Jesus. We could examine the classical creeds of the church, gaining valuable insight about the collective wisdom of the ages. We could restrict our study to contemporary theology in an attempt to study Jesus in light of our own culture. Or we could try our luck at our own creativity and produce yet another speculative view.

My choice is to look at Jesus as He is presented to us in the New Testament. Even if one rejects the revelatory character of the Bible or its divine inspiration, he must face one unassailable fact: virtually all we know about Jesus is recorded in the Scriptures. The New Testament writers are the primary sources of our knowledge of Jesus. If these sources are ignored or rejected, we are left with speculation and speculation alone.

We echo the cry of Erasmus, *"Ad fontes!"* ("To the sources!"), as we focus attention on the New Testament. No matter what advantages we may have from two thousand years of theological reflection, those years remove us from the virginal response of the contemporaries of Jesus who knew Him, who walked with Him, who observed Him in action, and who interpreted Him from the perspective of the Old Testament Scriptures. The biblical writers themselves are the primary sources, and it is their portrait of Jesus that must take priority in any serious study of this person. Outside of the New Testament writers, there are no more than three paragraphs of literature written in the first century about the person and work of Jesus.

When we go back to the biblical sources, we recognize that any attempt to understand Jesus must take into account the dangers imposed by our own minds. Though the New

Testament is not a product of the twenty-first century, those of us who read it today are. Each of us has had some exposure to the idea of Jesus since we were children, if from no other source than from the simple displays that we saw in Christmas crèches during the holiday season. Though we may not have an exhaustive knowledge of the biblical Jesus, we are not ignorant of Him either. Every literate American has some information about Jesus and some opinion about Him. Our opinions may or may not be in harmony with the biblical portrait, yet we bring those assumptions to the text and sometimes create an attitude of prejudice that makes it difficult for us to hear what Jesus' contemporaries were saying.

We also must be aware that Jesus is no mere figure of historical interest whom we can study dispassionately. We are aware of the claims that Jesus is the Son of God, the Savior of the world. We realize that we must make a decision about Him for or against. We are also aware that many believe such a decision determines one's eternal destiny. We sense that so much is at stake in our understanding of Jesus that we must approach the question not with indifference but with the understanding of who Jesus is. It is a question of ultimate significance to each one of us. Whether or not Jesus brings to my life an absolute claim is something I cannot intelligently ignore.

The New Testament writers give us an eyewitness account

of Jesus of Nazareth. Luke begins his Gospel with the following words:

> Inasmuch as many have undertaken to compile a narrative of the things that have been accomplished among us, just as those who from the beginning were eyewitnesses and ministers of the word have delivered them to us, it seemed good to me also, having followed all things closely for some time past, to write an orderly account for you, most excellent Theophilus, that you may have certainty concerning the things you have been taught. (Luke 1:1–4)

Peter adds the following statement:

> For we did not follow cleverly devised myths when we made known to you the power and coming of our Lord Jesus Christ, but we were eyewitnesses of his majesty. (2 Peter 1:16)

The biblical records claim to be firsthand accounts given to us by men who were self-consciously and openly committed to following Jesus. Let us look briefly at the testimony of those who knew Him, loved Him, and gave their lives for Him.

Chapter Two

THE TITLES
OF JESUS

A few years ago, a distinguished professor of New Testament was invited to address an academic convocation at a large seminary. A convocation in a university or seminary usually is attended with pomp and circumstance: The faculty members are adorned in full academic regalia as they march in procession to the front of the auditorium, and the guest speaker is expected to bring an address of weighty, scholarly material. Thus, on this occasion, when the New Testament professor entered the hall, there was a hush of expectancy as students and faculty waited with eager anticipation for his remarks. Being an expert in the field of Christology, the lecturer was expected to present an address revealing his most recent research in the field.

However, he stood at the lectern and began to recite a litany of the titles of Jesus drawn from the Scriptures. The litany went on for several minutes as the full impact of the titles, given without commentary, was felt by the audience. The professor stood and simply said with pauses in between: "Christ . . . Lord . . . Rabbi . . . Son of Man . . . Son of God . . . Son of David . . . Lion of Judah . . . the Rose of Sharon . . . the Bright and Morning Star . . . the Alpha and Omega . . . the Logos . . . the Advocate . . . the Prince of Peace . . . the only begotten of the Father . . . the Lamb without blemish. . . ." On and on it went as the man recited all of the titles that the biblical writers had conferred on Jesus.

These titles reveal something of His identity and give us a hint as to the meaning of His actions. It is customary in theology to distinguish between the person of Christ and the work of Christ. The distinction is an important one, but it must never involve a separation. Jesus is known in part by what He did. On the other hand, the significance of what He did is strongly conditioned by who He is. Though we may distinguish between person and work, we must never isolate the one from the other. When we look at the titles conferred on Jesus in the New Testament, we see an interplay between person and work.

Space does not permit an examination of all the titles ascribed to Jesus biblically, but let us examine briefly those that are generally considered His chief titles.

The Christ or the Messiah

The title Christ is so often used in conjunction with the name of Jesus that it has virtually become His name. One does not normally refer to Jesus as "Jesus bar Joseph" or even as "Jesus of Nazareth." Rather, His full name is considered to be "Jesus Christ." Because the term Christ is perceived to be a name, the full significance of it may be lost. Actually, Jesus is a name but Christ is a title. It is used more often than any other title for Jesus in the New Testament.

Christ comes from the Greek word *christos*, which means "anointed." It corresponds to the Hebrew word translated "messiah." When Jesus is called "Christ," He is being called "the Messiah." If we were to translate the name and the title directly into English, we would say "Jesus Messiah." With this title, we are making a confession of faith that

Jesus is the long-awaited anointed one of Israel, the Savior who would redeem His people.

In the Old Testament, the concept of the Messiah grew over a period of many years as God unfolded the character and role of the Messiah progressively. The term *messiah* initially meant "one anointed of God for a specific task." Anyone who was anointed to perform a work for God, such as a prophet, a priest, or a king, could be called "messiah" in the broad sense. Slowly, through the prophetic utterances of the Old Testament, a concept was developed of *the* Messiah, one who would be uniquely anointed of God to fulfill a divine task. When the New Testament writers ascribed the fulfillment of those prophecies to Jesus, they made a statement of tremendous importance. They were saying that Jesus was the one "who was to come." He fulfilled all the promises of God that converge in the person of the Messiah.

In the Old Testament, the concept of the Messiah is not a simple one, but has many nuances. There are different strands of messianic expectancy woven through the tapestry of these ancient books. At first glance, some of these appear contradictory. One of the main strands of messianic expectancy is the idea of a king like David who would restore the monarchy of Israel. There is a triumphant note in the expectation of a Messiah who would reign over Israel and put all enemies under His feet. This was the most popular variety of messianic expectancy at the time Jesus appeared on the scene. Israel had suffered since its conquest by the Romans and was bristling under the oppression of this alien yoke. A vast number of people were yearning for the fulfillment of the prophecies of the coming Messiah who would overthrow the Roman government and restore independence to Israel.

Another aspect of the concept of the Messiah was that of the Suffering Servant of Israel, the one who would bear the sins of the people. This notion is found most clearly in the Servant Songs of the prophet Isaiah, with Isaiah 53 being the chief text that the New Testament writers used to understand the ignominy of Jesus' death. The figure of a despised and rejected servant stands in stark contrast with the concept of a royal king.

A third strand of messianic expectancy is found in the so-called apocalyptic literature of the Old Testament, the highly symbolic writings of men such as Daniel and Ezekiel. Herein the Messiah, or Son of Man, is seen as a heavenly being who descends to earth in order to judge the world. It is difficult to conceive how one man could be both a heavenly being and an earthly king, a cosmic judge and a humiliated servant, at the same time. Yet these are the three major varieties of messianic expectancy that were very much alive at the time of Jesus' entrance to the world. In the following sections, I want to look more closely at these strands of expectancy.

The Son of David

The Old Testament reign of King David was the golden age of Israel. David excelled as a military hero and as a monarch. His military exploits extended the frontiers of the nation, and Israel emerged as a major world power and enjoyed great military strength and prosperity during his reign. But the golden age began to tarnish under Solomon's building program and turned to rust when the nation split under Jeroboam and Rehoboam. The memories of the great days lived on, however, in the history of the people. Nostalgia reached a peak under the oppression of the Roman Empire as the people of the land looked to God for a new David who would restore the former glory to Israel.

The expectation surrounding the hope of a political Messiah was not born simply from nostalgia, but had its roots in Old Testament prophecies that gave substance to such a dream. The Psalms declared that one like David would be anointed as king by God Himself. Psalm 132:11 says: "The LORD swore to David a sure oath from which he will not turn back: 'One of the sons of your body I will set on your throne.'" Psalm 89 declares: "I will establish his offspring forever and his throne as the days of the heavens. I will not violate my covenant, or alter the word that went forth from my lips. Once for all I have sworn by my holiness; I will not lie to David. His offspring shall endure for ever, his throne as long as the sun before me" (vv. 29, 34–36).

Not only in the Psalms but also in the Prophets we read of the future hopes for one like David. Amos, for example, proclaimed, "In that day I will raise up the booth of David that is fallen" (9:11).

These national hopes went through periods of fervor and dormancy in Israel, often depending on the degree of political freedom the nation enjoyed. In times of crisis and oppression, the flames of hope and expectancy were rekindled in the hearts of the people as they yearned for the restoration of David's fallen booth.

With the advent of Jesus, the notion of the fulfillment of the seed of David's royal Messiah was sparked afresh. It was not deemed a coincidence by the New Testament authors that Jesus came from the tribe of Judah, which had been promised the royal scepter by God. It was from the tribe of Judah, the tribe of David, that One was to come who would bring the new kingdom to Israel. The New Testament writers clearly saw the fulfillment of the Old Testament hope of a royal Messiah in the person of Jesus. This is seen in the central place of importance that the ascension of Jesus is given in the New Testament. Jesus is regarded as the Son of David who announces and inaugurates the kingdom of God.

There were times in Jesus' ministry when He had to flee from the multitudes who sought to make Him king because their views of kingship were so narrow. Theirs was a kingdom that would be inaugurated without the price of death and suffering. The crowds had little time for a king who was to suffer. Jesus had to withdraw from the crowds repeatedly, and He cautioned His disciples about declaring openly that He was the Messiah. At no point did He deny that He was the Christ. When His disciples boldly proclaimed their confidence in His messiahship, Jesus accepted the designation with His blessing.

The poignant moment of messianic unveiling took place at Caesarea Philippi, when Jesus asked His disciples: "Who do the crowds say that I am?" (Luke 9:18). The disciples told Jesus the scuttlebutt of the mobs: "Some say John the Baptist; others say Elijah, and others Jeremiah or one of the prophets." Finally Jesus put the question to His inner core of disciples: "But who do you say that I am?" Peter replied with fervency, "You are the Christ, the Son of the living God" (Matt. 16:14–16). Jesus' response to Peter's confession is pivotal to the New Testament understanding of the identity of Christ. Jesus replied: "Blessed are you, Simon Bar-Jonah! For flesh and blood has not revealed this to you, but my Father who is in heaven" (v. 17). Jesus pronounced His benediction on the one to whom God had revealed His true identity. He acknowledged that Peter's recognition of His identity was correct. It had not been gleaned from an examination of external manifestations; rather, Peter had recognized Jesus because the scales had been removed from his eyes by the revelation from God the Father.

On another occasion, John the Baptist greeted Jesus as "the Lamb of God, who takes away the sin of the world!" (John 1:29). But when John was arrested and cast into prison, his faith began to falter and he sent messengers to Jesus asking a pointed question: "Are you the one who is to come, or shall we look for another?" Jesus responded to the messengers by saying, "Go and tell John what you have seen and heard: the blind receive their sight, the lame walk, lepers are cleansed, and the deaf hear, and the dead are raised up, the poor have good news preached to them"

(Luke 7:20–22). These words were not idly chosen. Jesus was calling attention to the prophecy of Isaiah 61, the text that He had read the day He entered the synagogue in Nazareth: "The Spirit of the Lord is upon me, because He has anointed me to proclaim good news to the poor. He has sent me to proclaim liberty to the captives and recovering of sight to the blind, to set at liberty those who are oppressed, to proclaim the year of the Lord's favor" (Luke 4:18–19). After He finished reading the scroll, Jesus said, "Today this scripture has been fulfilled in your hearing" (v. 21). Essentially, Jesus' reply to the message of John was this: "Tell John to read again the prophecies of Isaiah, and he will know the answer to his question."

The Suffering Servant of Israel

The figure of the Servant of the Lord or "the Suffering Servant" spoken of by the prophet Isaiah is normative to the New Testament understanding of Jesus. Debates rage as to the identity of the author of Isaiah and the identity of the Servant in the author's mind. Some argue that the Servant referred to Israel corporately, while others apply the role to Cyrus, and some to Isaiah himself. This debate will surely continue, but the fact that the New Testament authors found the ultimate fulfillment of this figure in Jesus is beyond dispute.

It is also clear that Jesus thought of His own ministry in terms of Isaiah's prophecy, as we have seen from His statement in the synagogue and from His reply to John the Baptist's inquiry.

It is not by accident that Isaiah is the most frequently quoted prophet in the New Testament. Prophecies from Isaiah quoted in the New Testament are not limited to Jesus' suffering, but refer to Jesus' entire ministry. It was the death of Christ, however, that riveted the attention of the New Testament authors to the Servant prophecies of Isaiah. Let's look at Isaiah 53:

Who has believed what he has heard from us?
And to whom has the arm of the LORD been revealed?
For he grew up before him like a young plant,
and like a root out of dry ground;
he had no form or majesty that we should look at him,
and no beauty that we should desire him.
He was despised and rejected by men;
a man of sorrows, and acquainted with grief;
and as one from whom men hide their faces
he was despised, and we esteemed him not.

Surely he has borne our griefs
and carried our sorrows;
yet we esteemed him stricken,
smitten by God, and afflicted.
But he was wounded for our transgressions;
he was crushed for our iniquities;
upon him was the chastisement that brought us peace,
and with his stripes we are healed.
All we like sheep have gone astray;
we have turned—every one—to his own way;
and the LORD has laid on him
the iniquity of us all.

He was oppressed, and he was afflicted,
yet he opened not his mouth;
like a lamb that is led to the slaughter,
and like a sheep that before its shearers is silent,
so he opened not his mouth.
By oppression and judgment he was taken away;
and as for his generation, who considered
that he was cut off out of the land of the living,
stricken for the transgression of my people?
And they made his grave with the wicked
and with a rich man in his death,

although he had done no violence,
and there was no deceit in his mouth.

Yet it was the will of the LORD to crush him;
he has put him to grief;
when his soul makes an offering for guilt,
he shall see his offspring; he shall prolong his days;
the will of the LORD shall prosper in his hand.
Out of the anguish of his soul he shall see and be
    satisfied;
by his knowledge shall the righteous one, my servant,
make many to be accounted righteous,
and he shall bear their iniquities.
Therefore I will divide him a portion with the many,
and he shall divide the spoil with the strong,
because he poured out his soul to death
and was numbered with the transgressors;
yet he bore the sin of many,
and makes intercession for the transgressors.

Repeated study of Isaiah 53 augments rather than
diminishes our astonishment at its content. It reads like an
eyewitness account of the passion of Jesus. Here the princi-
ples of corporate solidarity and imputation of sin are clearly

demonstrated. The scandal of Jesus is found in the centrality of His suffering as the way of redemption. The Messiah comes not only as King, but as a Servant who receives the chastisement for the iniquity of the people. In this, the one dies for the many. Any interpretation of the life and work of Jesus that fails to take this aspect seriously does radical violence to the text of the New Testament.

That the concepts of the royal King of Israel and the Suffering Servant of Israel were merged in one man is seen dramatically in the heavenly vision that unfolded before the apostle John on the Isle of Patmos. In one part of the vision, John was given a glimpse behind the veil of heaven. He heard the cry of the angel, "Who is worthy to open the scroll and break its seals?" (Rev. 5:2). John reports with subdued emotion that no one was found worthy of the task. His disappointment gave way to grief: "I began to weep loudly because no one was found worthy to open the scroll or to look into it" (5:4). At that point, an elder consoled him, saying, "Weep no more; behold, the Lion of the tribe of Judah, the Root of David, has conquered, so that he can open the scroll and its seven seals" (5:5). An abrupt and marked change in the mood of the narrative follows, as a sense of excited expectancy replaces the atmosphere of despair. John awaits the appearance of the triumphal Lion.

The irony is completed when John sees not the Lion but a slain Lamb standing in the midst of the elders. He records that the Lamb took the scroll from the right hand of Him who was seated on the throne, and thousands of angels sang, "Worthy is the Lamb who was slain, to receive . . . honor and glory and blessing!" (5:12). Here the Lion and the Lamb are one and the same person. The Servant reigns as King.

The Son of Man

At the Council of Chalcedon in the fifth century, the Christian church sought to find a formula that would call attention both to the full humanity of Jesus and to His full deity. The words the church settled on in A.D. 451 were *"vere homo, vere Deus."* The formula meant that Jesus was truly man and truly God, calling attention to His two natures.

In the New Testament, we find that Jesus is called both the Son of Man and the Son of God. These two titles appearing in this way offer a strong temptation to assume that "Son of God" refers exclusively to Jesus' deity and "Son of Man" refers exclusively to His humanity. However, approaching these titles in this way would lead us into very serious error.

With the title *Son of Man*, we stumble on something strange and fascinating. This is the third-most-frequently-used title for Jesus in the New Testament. It occurs eighty-four times, eighty-one of them in the four Gospels. In almost every case in which we find the title, it is used by Jesus to describe Himself. Thus, though it is only third in order of frequency of the titles that describe Jesus in the New Testament, it is number one with respect to Jesus' self-designation. It was obviously His favorite title for Himself. This is evidence of the integrity of the biblical writers in preserving a title for Jesus that they themselves chose so infrequently. They must have been tempted to put their own favorite titles in Jesus' mouth. It is commonplace in our day to argue that the biblical portrait of Jesus is merely the creation of the early church, rather than an accurate reflection of the historic Jesus. If this were the case, it would be extremely unlikely that the early church would put into Jesus' mouth a title they almost never used themselves to describe Him.

Why did Jesus use the title *Son of Man*? Some assume that it was because of humility—that He shunned more exalted titles and selected this one as a humble means of identifying with lowly humanity. Certainly there is an element of that identification in it, but this title also appears in the Old Testament, and its function there is anything but a humble one. References to the figure of the Son of Man are found in Daniel, Ezekiel, and some extrabiblical writings of rabbinic Judaism. Though scholars disagree, the historic consensus is that Jesus adopted the meaning of the term *Son of Man* as it is found in Daniel's visionary work.

In the book of Daniel, the Son of Man appears in a vision of heaven. He is presented before the throne of the "Ancient of Days" and is given "dominion and glory and a kingdom, that all peoples, nations, and languages should serve him; his dominion is an everlasting dominion, which shall not pass away, and his kingdom one that shall not be destroyed" (Dan. 7:14). Here the Son of Man is a heavenly being, a transcendent figure who will descend to the earth to exercise the role of supreme judge.

The testimony in the New Testament to the preexistence of Jesus is inseparably linked to the Son of Man motif. He is the one who is sent from the Father. The theme of the *descent* of Christ is the basis for His ascension. "No one has ascended into heaven except he who descended from heaven, the Son of Man" (John 3:13).

It is not enough to declare that the New Testament writers confessed Jesus was a heavenly being. Jesus was not just any heavenly being—angels are heavenly beings, but they are not like Jesus. He was described in language restricted to deity alone.

It is interesting to compare the graphic description of Daniel's vision of the Ancient of Days with John's description of the Son of Man in the book of Revelation. Here is Daniel's description of the Ancient of Days:

> "As I looked,
> thrones were placed,
> and the Ancient of Days took his seat;
> his clothing was white as snow,
> and the hair of his head like pure wool;
> his throne was fiery flames;
> its wheels were burning fire.
> A stream of fire issued
> and came out from before him;
> a thousand thousands served him,
> and ten thousand times ten thousand stood before him;
> the court sat in judgment,
> and the books were opened." (Dan. 7:9–10)

By comparison, here is John's description of the exalted Son of Man:

Then I turned to see the voice that was speaking to me, and on turning I saw seven golden lampstands, and in the midst of the lampstands one like a son of man, clothed with a long robe and with a golden sash around his chest. The hairs of his head were white, like white wool, like snow. His eyes were like a flame of fire, his feet were like burnished bronze, refined in a furnace, and his voice was like the roar of many waters. In his right hand he held seven stars, from his mouth came a sharp two-edged sword, and his face was like the sun shining in full strength. . . . Then I looked, and I heard around the throne and the living creatures and the elders the voice of many angels, numbering myriads of myriads and thousands of thousands, saying with a loud voice, "Worthy is the Lamb who was slain, to receive power and wealth and wisdom and might and honor and glory and blessing!" (Rev. 1:12–16; 5:11–12)

That the Son of Man was a figure of splendor and power cannot be missed. His deity is seen not only in the Old Testament portrait, but in Jesus' understanding as well. Jesus linked the Son of Man with creation by saying, "The Son of Man is lord even of the Sabbath" (Mark 2:28). To claim lordship over the Sabbath is to claim it over creation. The Sabbath was not merely a piece of Sinaitic legislation but a creation ordinance given by the Lord of Creation. Jesus also said, "That you may know that the Son of Man has authority on earth to forgive sins . . ." (Luke 5:24). Here, Jesus claimed an authority that, to the Jew, was a prerogative of God alone. The Jews did not miss the inference of these claims. They sought to kill Jesus precisely because His claims to deity came through loud and clear. The Son of Man came from heaven to judge the world. He would separate the sheep from the goats; He would come in clouds of glory at the end of the age.

The Son of Man who comes from heaven, however, is not one who is exclusively deity, but one who enters into our humanity through incarnation. It is probable that Paul's concept of Jesus as the second Adam was an elaboration of the Son of Man motif.

In addition to the titles that came from these three strands of expectancy—Son of David, Suffering Servant, Son of Man—the New Testament uses a number of other titles for Jesus. Let us now look more closely at some of these.

Jesus as Lord

We have seen that *Christ* is the most-often-used title for Jesus in the New Testament. The second-most-frequent designation for Him is *Lord*. So important is this title to the biblical understanding of Jesus that it became an integral part of the earliest Christian creed, the simple statement, "Jesus is Lord." *Lord* is the most exalted title conferred on Jesus.

Sometimes it is difficult for people in the United States to grasp the full significance of the title *Lord*. An Englishman of my acquaintance came to this country in the 1960s and spent his first week in Philadelphia visiting historic landmarks such as Independence Hall and the Liberty Bell in order to familiarize himself with American culture. He also visited several antique stores that specialized in Colonial and Revolutionary memorabilia. In one such shop, he saw several posters and signboards that contained slogans of the Revolution such as "No Taxation Without Representation" and "Don't Tread on Me." One signboard particularly attracted his attention. In bold letters, the sign proclaimed: "WE SERVE NO SOVEREIGN HERE." As he mused on this sign, he wondered how people steeped in such an antimonarchical culture could come to grips with the notion of the kingdom of God and the sovereignty that belongs to the Lord. The concept of lordship invested in one individual is repugnant to the American tradition, yet the New Testament boldly makes this claim for Jesus, asserting that absolute sovereign authority and imperial power are vested in Him.

The New Testament synonym for *lord* is the Greek word *kurios*. That word was used in several ways in the ancient world. In its most common usage, it functioned as a polite word for *sir*. Just as our English word *sir* can be used in an ordinary sense and in a special sense, so it was with *kurios*. In England, men who are knighted are given the title *sir*, and in that instance the word moves from the common use to the formal.

A second use of *kurios* in the Greek culture was as a title given to men of the aristocratic class who were slave owners. This title was used figuratively for Jesus throughout the New Testament, where He is called "Master" by His disciples. Paul frequently introduced his epistles by saying, "Paul, a *slave* of Jesus Christ." The word he used is *doulos*. There could not be a slave (*doulos*) without a lord (*kurios*). Paul declared, "You are not your own, for you were bought with a price" (1 Cor. 6:19–20). Here the believer is seen as a possession of Jesus. Jesus owns His people. He is not a despot or tyrant, as we might expect in an earthly slave/master situation. The irony of New Testament lordship is that only in slavery to Christ can a man discover authentic freedom. The irony is pushed further by the New Testament teaching that it is through a slave/master relationship to Jesus that a person is liberated from bondage in this world. This twist in teaching is found particularly in the writings of the apostle Paul.

The third and most important meaning of *kurios* was the imperial usage. Here the title was given to one who had absolute sovereignty over a group of people. It is a usage that was usually understood politically.

Perhaps the most striking aspect of the title *Lord* was its relationship to the Old Testament. The Greek translation of the Old Testament used the word *kurios* to translate the Hebrew word *adonai*, a title used for God. The sacred name of God, Yahweh, was unspoken, often replaced in the liturgy of Israel with another word. When a substitute was used for the ineffable name of God, the usual selection was *adonai*, a title that called attention to God's absolute rule over the earth.

In many versions of the Bible, both *Yahweh* and *adonai* are translated by the English word *Lord*, though a distinction between them is found in the method of printing. When *Yahweh* is translated, the word is usually printed with a large capital letter followed by small capitals: "LORD." When *adonai* is the Hebrew word, it is printed "Lord." Psalm 8, for example, begins: "O LORD, our Lord, how majestic is your name in all the earth!" The Hebrew would be: "O Yahweh, our adonai, how majestic. . . ." Here, *Yahweh* functions as the name of God and *adonai* is used as a title.

One Old Testament passage that is quoted frequently in the New Testament is Psalm 110. Here we find something strange indeed. Psalm 110 reads, "The LORD says to my Lord: 'Sit at my right hand!'" Yahweh speaks to Adonai, who is seen as David's Lord and is seated at God's right hand. In the New Testament, Jesus is the one who is elevated to the right hand of God and receives the title *Lord*. This is the title that is "above every name" and is conferred on Jesus at His ascension. Jesus, being seated at the right hand of God, is elevated to the seat of cosmic authority where all authority in heaven and earth is given into His hands, and He receives the title *Adonai* that formerly had been restricted to God the Father. The exalted nature of the title can be seen not only from this context, but also from usage in its superlative form. When Jesus is called "Lord of lords," there is no doubt what is meant.

The title *Lord* is so central to the life of the New Testament Christian community that the English word *church* derives from it. The Greek word for *church* is *ekklesia*, which is brought over into English in the word *ecclesiastical*. The English word *church* is similar in sound and form to other languages' word for church: *kirk* in Scotland, *kerk* in Holland, and *kirche* in Germany all derive from the same root. That source is the Greek word *kuriache*, which means "those who belong to the *kurios*." Thus, *church* in its literal origin means "the people who belong to the Lord."

One puzzling note in the New Testament is this statement, "No one can say 'Jesus is Lord' except in the Holy Spirit" (1 Cor. 12:3). Some have pointed to this as a contradiction because Jesus says on other occasions that people do in fact profess that He is Lord without meaning it. Jesus concludes the Sermon on the Mount with the somber warning, "On that day many will say to me, 'Lord, Lord.' . . . And then I will declare to them, 'I never knew you; depart from me'" (Matt. 7:22–23). Since it is evident that people can honor Christ with their lips while their hearts are far from Him, so that they can speak the words "Jesus is Lord," what does the Bible mean when it says, "No one can say 'Jesus is Lord' except in the Holy Spirit"?

There are two ways in which we can answer this question. The first would be by asserting what is tacitly understood in the text but left unspoken. That is, no one can say that Jesus is Lord and *mean it* except in the Holy Spirit. That would be sound theology, and we have literary license to fill in the unstated qualifier. However, there may be something more concrete in view here. At the time the text was written, Christians were considered enemies of the established order of Rome and guilty of treason for their refusal to subscribe to the cult of emperor worship. The test for loyalty to the empire was the public recitation of the words "*Kaiser kurios*" ("Caesar is lord"). Christians refused to recite this oath, even when it cost them their lives. When they were called on to utter it, they would substitute "*Iesous ho Kurios*" ("Jesus is Lord"). Christians were willing to pay their taxes, to give honor to Caesar where honor was due, to render to Caesar those things that were Caesar's. However, the exalted title *Lord* belonged to Jesus alone, and Christians paid with their lives to maintain that assertion. The statement in the biblical text, "No one can say 'Jesus is Lord' except in the Holy Spirit," may have referred to the fact that in those days people hesitated to make such a bold statement publicly unless they were prepared to take the consequences.

The Son of God

The New Testament recounts few instances when God was heard speaking from heaven. When He did, it was normally to announce something startling. God was zealous to announce that Jesus Christ was His Son. At Jesus' baptism, the heavens opened and God's voice was heard, saying, "This is my beloved Son, with whom I am well pleased" (Matt. 3:17). Elsewhere, the Father declared from heaven, "This is my beloved Son; listen to him" (Mark 9:7). Thus, the title conferred from on high to Jesus is *Son of God*.

This title has engendered a great deal of controversy in the history of the church, particularly in the fourth century, when the Arian movement, taking its cue from its leader, Arius, denied the Trinity by arguing that Jesus was a created being. References to Jesus as "the firstborn of all creation" (Col. 1:15) and "the only begotten of the Father" (John 1:14, KJV) led Arius to argue that Jesus had a beginning in time and was thus a creature. In Arias' mind, if Jesus was begotten, it could only mean that He was not eternal, and if He was not eternal, then He was a creature. Thus, to ascribe deity to Jesus was to be guilty of blasphemy, because it involved the idolatrous worship of a created being. The same controversy exists today between Christian believers and the Mormons and Jehovah's Witnesses, both of whom acknowledge a lofty view of Jesus over angels and other creatures but deny His full deity.

This controversy precipitated in the great ecumenical

Council of Nicea. The Nicene Creed provides an interesting answer to the charges of Arianism. The answer is found in the strange statement that Jesus is "begotten, not made." To the Greek, such a statement was a contradiction in terms. In normal terms, *begotten* implies a beginning, but when applied to Jesus, there is a uniqueness to the way in which He is begotten that separates Him from all other creatures. Jesus is called the *monogenes*, the "only begotten" of the Father. There is a sense in which Jesus and Jesus alone is begotten of the Father. This is what the church was getting at when it spoke of Jesus being eternally begotten—that He was begotten, not made.

This uniqueness is found not only in Jesus' eternal character, but also in the fact that Jesus' sonship carries with it a description of intimacy with the Father. The primary significance of sonship in the New Testament is in its figurative reference to obedience. Thus, to be a son of God biblically is to be one who is in a unique relationship of obedience to the will of God. Likewise, the motif of the firstborn has more to do with preeminence than with biology. The term *begotten* is a Greek word filled with Jewish content. Nicea was not flirting with irrationality, but was being faithful to Scripture by using the strange-sounding formula "begotten, not made."

The Logos

The title *Logos* is rarely used in the New Testament for Jesus. We find it prominently in the prologue to the Gospel of John, where we read, "In the beginning was the Word [*Logos*], and the Word was with God, and the Word was God." In spite of its infrequent use, this title became the focal point of the theological development of the Christian church's understanding of Jesus in the first three or four centuries of church history. It was the dominant concept by which the theologians of the church considered their doctrine of Jesus. The great minds of Alexandria, of Antioch, of East and West, poured themselves into an exhaustive study of the meaning of this title. There were significant reasons for that. The title lends itself, perhaps more than any other, to deep philosophical and theological speculation. That is precisely because the word *logos* was already a loaded term, pregnant with meaning against the background of Greek philosophy.

As in the case with other titles we have considered, there is a common meaning and a more technical meaning to *logos*. The common meaning for the word is simply "word, thought, or concept." English translations of the New Testament normally translate *logos* as "word." However, from the prologue of John we see that *logos* had an exalted meaning as well. The word *logic* in English derives from *logos*, as does the suffix *–ology*, which often is attached to words designating academic disciplines and sciences. For instance, theology is "theoslogos," a word or concept of God. Biology is "bioslogos," a word or concept of life.

One Christian philosopher, Gordon H. Clark, has suggested that the early verses of John's Gospel could be fittingly translated as follows: "In the beginning was logic, and logic was with God and God was logic . . . and the logic became flesh." Such a translation may raise the hackles of Christians because it seems to represent a crass form of rationalism, reducing the eternal Christ to a mere rational principle. However, that is not what Dr. Clark had in mind here. He was simply saying that in God Himself there is a coherence, unity, consistency, and symmetry by which all things in this world hold together under His rule. God expresses this principle of coherency that comes from within His own being by His Word, which is itself coherent, consistent, and symmetrical. Christ is identified with the eternal *Logos* within God Himself, which brings order and harmony to the created world.

This principle of coherency forms the link between John's Christianized view of the *Logos* and the concept that was found in ancient Greek philosophy. The ancient Greeks were preoccupied with finding the ultimate meaning of the universe and the stuff from which everything was made. They perceived the vast diversity of created things and sought some point of unity that would make sense of it all. As in the case of Greek art, the thinkers of the day abhorred chaos and confusion. They wanted to understand life in a unified way. Thus, in many theories of philosophy that came before the writing of the New Testament, the Greek word *logos* functioned as an important concept. We think for example of Heraclitus, an early Greek philosopher, who is still revered by many as the patron saint of modern existentialism. Heraclitus had a theory that everything was in a state of change and that all things were composed ultimately of some form of fire. However, Heraclitus required some explanation for the origin and root of things, and he located that in an abstract theory of a *logos*.

We find the same concept in Stoic philosophy and even earlier in pre-Socratic philosophy. In early Greek thought, there was no concept of a transcendent personal God who created the world in order and harmony by His wisdom and sovereignty. At best, there was speculation about an abstract principle that ordered reality and kept it from becoming a blur of confusion. This abstract principle they called a "*nous*" (which means "mind") or the "*logos*," an impersonal, philosophical principle. The concept of *logos* was never considered as a personal being who would become involved with the things of this world; the idea functioned merely as an abstraction necessary to account for the order evident in the universe.

The Stoics whom Paul debated at Mars Hill had a notion that all things were composed of an ultimate seminal fire, which they called the *Logos Spermatikos*. This referred to the seminal word, the word that contains procreative power, the word that begets life and order and harmony. We have all heard the expression, "Every person has a spark of divinity in him." This notion did not originate from Christianity but from the Stoics. The Stoics believed that every individual object had a piece of the divine seminal fire in it, but again, the *logos* in the Stoic concept remained impersonal and abstract.

By the time the Gospels were written, the notion of *logos* was a loaded philosophical category. The apostle John dropped a theological bombshell on the philosophical playground of his day by looking at Jesus and talking about Him not as an impersonal concept but as the incarnation of the eternal *Logos*. He did not use the term in the same way that the Greeks did, but he baptized it and filled it with a Jewish-Christian meaning. For John, the *Logos* was intensely personal and radically different from that which was found in Greek speculative philosophy. The *Logos* was a person, not a principle.

The second scandal to the Greek mind was that the *Logos* should become incarnate. For the ancient Greek, nothing was more of a stumbling block than the idea of incarnation. Because the Greeks had a dualistic view of spirit and matter, it was unthinkable that God, if He really existed, should ever take on Himself human flesh. This world of material things was viewed as being intrinsically imperfect, and for the *Logos* to clothe Himself in the garb of a material world would be abhorrent to anyone steeped in classical Greek philosophy. The apostle John, under the inspiration of the Holy Spirit, looked at the personal, historical Christ and saw in Him the manifestation of the eternal person by whose transcendent power all things hold together. This concept, perhaps more than any other, gave clear attention to the deity of Christ in His total cosmic significance. He is the *Logos* that created the heaven and the earth. He is the transcendent power behind the universe. He is the ultimate reality of all things.

John said the *Logos* is not only with God, He *is* God. There is no more direct statement or more clear affirmation of the deity of Christ to be found anywhere in Scripture than in the first verse of John's Gospel. The Greek literally reads, "God was the Word" (usually translated in English as "The Word was God"). Modern Jehovah's Witnesses and Mormons have tried to obviate this passage by clever distortions. Some of their translations change the text and simply say, "The Word was like God." The Greeks had a word for "like" that is found nowhere in this text of John. The simple structure, "God was the Word," can mean only an identification between Jesus and deity. Another way the Mormons and Jehovah's Witnesses seek to get around this passage is by arguing that the definite article is not present in the text. They assert that since the Bible does not say the Word was *the* God, it simply says the Word *was* God, and that this does not carry with it the weight of an affirmation of deity. Thus, we would be left with the statement that the Word was "a god." If that was what John was trying to communicate, the problems that this solution raises are greater than those it solves. It leaves us with John affirming a crass kind of polytheism. In the context of biblical literature, it is clear that there is but one God. The Bible is monotheistic from the beginning to the end. The absence or presence of the definite article has no theological significance whatsoever in this text.

There is some difficulty with the text in that the Word is said to be both *with* God and to *be* God. Here we find that the Word is both distinguished from God and identified with God. It is because of texts such as this that the church found it necessary to formulate its doctrine of God in terms of the Trinity. We must see a sense in which Christ is the same as God the Father and yet be able to distinguish Him from the Father. The idea of distinguishing and yet identifying is not something that is an intrusion on the New Testament text but a distinction that texts such as John 1 demand. The Father and the Son are one being, yet distinguished in terms of personality as well as by the work and ministry they perform.

In the first chapter of John, the idea of the *Logos* being "with" God is significant. The Greek language has three words that can be translated by the English word *with*. The first is *sun*, which is rendered in English as the prefix *syn*. We find it in words such as *synchronize, syncretism, synagogue,* and so on. A synagogue, for example, is a place where people come together with other people. To "be with" in the sense of *sun* is to be present in a group, to be gathered with other people. This refers to a collection of people.

The second word that can be translated by the English word *with* is *meta*, which means "to be alongside." When we think of people being alongside each other we think of them standing side by side. If I were to walk down the street side by side with a person, I would be with him in the sense of *meta*.

The Greek language has a third word that can be translated "with," and it is *pros*. This is found less frequently than the others, but it is in the root word for another Greek word, *prosepone*, which means "face." This kind of "withness" is the most intimate of all types. John is saying here that the *Logos* existed with God, *pros* God, that is, face to face in a relationship of eternal intimacy. This was the kind of relationship the Old Testament Hebrew yearned to have with his God. The *Logos* enjoys this kind of intimate, face-to-face relationship with the Father from all eternity. The Father and Son are one in their relationship as well as in their being.

In John's prologue (1:1–14), the concept of the *Logos* comes to a climax as we read, "And the Word became flesh and dwelt among us . . . we have seen his glory, glory as of the only Son from the Father." The word translated "dwelt" here literally means to "pitch his tent among us." Even as God dwelt with the people of Israel in the Old Testament by means of a tabernacle, so the New Testament tabernacle is the incarnate Word, the *Logos* who embodies the truth of

God Himself. He is the mind of God made flesh, coming to dwell with us in flesh and blood. When He makes His appearance, it is a manifestation of glory. As John tells us, "In him was life, and the life was the light of men" (1:4).

Jesus as Savior

There are other titles of note ascribed to Jesus. He is the Rabbi, the second Adam, the Mediator. But no title captures His work more completely than Savior. The believers of the early church bore witness to this when they used the sign of the fish as their cryptic signal of identification. The acrostic formed by the letters of the Greek word for "fish" stands for "Jesus Christ, Son of God, Savior."

God Himself named Jesus as an infant. *Jesus* means "the Lord saves" or "the one through whom the Lord saves." Thus, Jesus' own name carries within it the idea of savior. His titles—*Logos, Messiah, Son of Man*—all indicate Jesus' qualifications to be the Savior of men. He alone has the credentials to offer atonement, to triumph over death, to reconcile people to God.

Here is where the relevance of Jesus crashes into our lives, bringing crisis. Here is where we step over the line of detached scholarly investigation and into the realm of personal vulnerability. We argue endlessly over matters of religion and philosophy, about ethics and politics, but each person must ultimately face the personal issue squarely: "What do I do about my sin?"

That I sin and that you sin is debated by none save the most dishonest of men. We sin. We violate each other. We assault the holiness of God. What hope do we have in such dreadful turmoil? We can deny our sin or even the existence of God. We can exclaim that we are not accountable for our lives. We can invent a God who forgives everybody without requiring repentance. All such avenues are established in delusion. There is but one who qualifies as Savior. He alone has the ability to solve our most abysmal dilemma. He alone has the power of life and death.

The titles of Jesus tell us who He is. Contained in them, however, is a thesaurus of insights into what He did. His person and His work meet in the drama of life. We move now to a consideration of the chronology of His career, highlighting those episodes in which person and work merged in the divine/human plan of redemption.

Chapter Three

THE LIFE OF JESUS

The records of Jesus' life and ministry cause controversy from the very start. The extraordinary narrative of the circumstances surrounding His conception and birth provokes howls of protest from the critics of supernaturalism. They must begin their work of demythologizing early, wielding scissors on the first page of the New Testament. Following Matthew's table of genealogy, the first paragraph of the first Gospel reads as follows: "Now the birth of Jesus Christ took place in this way. When his mother Mary had been betrothed to Joseph, before they came together she was found to be with child from the Holy Spirit" (Matt. 1:18).

Though the New Testament is replete with miracles surrounding the person of Jesus, none seems more offensive to modern man than the virgin birth. If any law of science is established as immutable and unbreakable, it is that human reproduction is not possible without the conjoining of the male seed and the female egg. We may have developed sophisticated methods of artificial insemination and "test-tube" intrauterine implantations, but in some manner the reproduction process requires the contribution of both genders of the race to succeed.

Thus, the birth of Jesus violates the inviolable; it mutates the immutable; it breaks the unbreakable. It is alleged to be an act that is pure and simple *contra naturam*. Before we even read of the activities of Jesus' life, we are thrust headfirst against this claim. Many skeptics close the door on further investigation after reading the first page of the record. The story sounds too much like magic, too much like the sort of myth and legend that tends to grow up around the portraits of famous people.

The arguments against the virgin birth are many. They range from the charge of borrowing mythical baggage from the Greek-speaking world, with parallels evident in pagan mythology (Ovid's *Metamorphosis* is cited as "Exhibit A"), to the scientific disclaimer that the virgin birth represents an empirically unverifiable unique event that denies all probability quotients. Some have offered a desperate exegetical argument trying to show that the New Testament doesn't teach the idea of virgin birth. This we call the exegesis of despair.

The real problem is that of miracle. It doesn't stop with the birth of Jesus but follows Him through His life, ministry, death, resurrection, and ascension. The life of Jesus carries the aura of miracle wherever it is described in the primary sources. A "de-miraclized" Jesus is not the biblical Jesus, but the invention of those who cannot abide the biblical proclamation. Such a Jesus is the Jesus of unbelief, the most mythical Jesus of all, conjured up to fit the preconceived molds of unbelief.

Behind the problem of miracle are certain assumptions about the reality of God the Creator. Matthew's infancy narrative raises questions not only about parthenogenesis but about genesis itself. Creation is the unique event to beat all unique events. It's not so amazing that a God who has the power to bring the universe into being from nothing (*ex nihilo*)—without preexistent matter to work with, without means, but by the sheer omnipotent power of His voice—can also produce the birth of a baby by supernaturally fertilizing a material egg in a woman's womb. What defies logic is that a host of theologians grant the former but deny the latter. They allow the supernatural birth of the whole but deny the possibility of the part. We have to ask the painful question: Do they really believe in God in the first place, or is espoused belief in the Creator merely a societal convention, a veil to a more fundamental unbelief?

The Ironclad Law of Causality

Perhaps the most ironclad law of nature is the law of causality. Effects require causes. If the universe is an effect, in whole or in part, then it requires a cause that is sufficient to the effect. The cause may be greater than its effect, but it certainly cannot be lesser. Modern science has not repealed the law of causality, though some injudicious thinkers have sought to do so when prejudice requires it. The other option to causality is that something comes from nothing—no cause is asserted: no material cause, no efficient cause, no sufficient cause, no formal cause, no final cause. Such a theory is not science but magic. No, it cannot even be magic; magic requires a magician. The law that something cannot come from nothing (*ex nihilo nihil fit*) remains unassailable.

Does not Christianity assert a universe that comes from nothing? Do we not assert an *ex nihilo* creation? Indeed we do. However, that "nothing" has reference to the absence of a *material* cause. There is a *sufficient* cause for the universe. There is an *efficient* cause for the universe. There is a God who has within Himself the power to create. God has the power of being within Himself. Such an assertion is not gratuitous, nor is it the mere dogmatic assertion of religion. It is a dictate of science and reason. If something *is*, then something intrinsically has the power of being. Somewhere, somehow, something must have the power of being. If not, we are left with only two options: (1) being comes from nothing or (2) nothing is (a contradiction). These options would be more miraculous than miracles if such were possible.

Some seek to escape the dilemma by pointing to the universe itself or to some undiscovered part of it as the eternal source of being. They try to explain the present world by saying that a supernatural or transcendent being is not required to account for the presence of being. To argue in this manner is to slip into a serious confusion of language. The universe daily exhibits effects. Nature changes. The very meaning of *super*nature or *transcendence* refers to questions of being. A being is said to be transcendent not because it is spatially or geographically located on the far side of Mars but because it has a special power of being—a higher order of being—defined precisely as that which has the power of being within itself. Wherever or whatever it is is beside the point. I know it does not reside in me. I am not it. My very existence depends on it—without it I pass into nothing. I know I am an effect and so was my mother and her mother before her. If we retrace the problem infinitely, we compound the problem infinitely. Modern man strains out the gnat and swallows the camel when he thinks he can have an existing world without a self-existing God.

The question of the virgin birth is not so much a philosophical question as it is a historical one. If one whom we call God has the power of being—sovereign efficient and sufficient causal power—then we cannot rationally object to the virgin birth on the grounds that it couldn't happen.

The real issue is not *could* it happen but *did* it happen. It becomes then a question of history and drives us once again to the historical sources. Those sources must be accepted or rejected on the basis of their credibility, a credibility that may not be predetermined by philosophical prejudice. The purpose of this chapter is not primarily to assess the veracity of these historical sources—that requires a separate work— but to rehearse their content that we may examine the only historical portrait of Jesus we have.

The Birth of Jesus

Matthew begins with a sober and bold declaration: "Now the birth of Jesus Christ took place *in this way*" (Matt. 1:18, emphasis added). Matthew purports to tell us not only what happened but how it happened.

Matthew focuses sharply on the extraordinary character of Jesus' birth, capturing the agony of Joseph's consternation. Joseph was a simple man, not privy to the sophisticated technology of our day. He knew nothing of *in vitro* fertilization and was unfamiliar with debates about parthenogenesis. He did not understand the simple rules of biology that are common knowledge to today's tenth-grade student. He lived in a prescientific age in a prescientific community. Still, Joseph did not have to be a skilled biologist to know that babies don't come from the stork. We must remember that virgin births were as rare in the first century as they are in the twenty-first.

Joseph was vulnerable *in extremis*. He had committed his life to Mary, trusting her purity in a society where adultery was scandalous. His betrothed came to him with a crushing revelation: "Joseph, I am pregnant." Mary then proceeded to explain her condition by telling Joseph that she had been visited by an angel who declared that she would be with child by the Holy Spirit. Joseph responded by tenderly considering "to divorce her quietly." There is no evidence of acrimony or furious rage by Joseph. He chose not to have her stoned, but began thinking of ways to protect Mary from the consequences of her delusions.

It is clear from the biblical text that Joseph was the first hard-core skeptic of the virgin birth—until an angel visited him and made him a convert to the "delusion." Nothing else would do. What man would believe such a story with less than miraculous evidence to attest it?

The road from Jesus' conception to His birth, from Zechariah, Elizabeth, Mary, and Joseph to the shepherds outside Bethlehem, was surrounded by angels. They appeared at every turn, saturating the event with the supernatural.

With the activity of angels in full play, the critic works overtime with his scissors. He needs an electric knife to do the job, as angels appear at the birth, the temptation, the resurrection, and the ascension of Jesus. They are promised as part of the retinue of His return. The words *angel* or *angels* appear more frequently in the New Testament than the word *sin*. They appear more often than the word *love*. Put the scissors to angels and you are engaged, not in biblical criticism, but in biblical vandalism.

Pilgrims flock daily to the sacred sites of the life of Jesus.

They follow the route of the *Via Dolorosa*; they argue about the authentic site of Golgotha and the garden tomb. Modern mountains compete for recognition as the locus of the Sermon on the Mount. Yet the field outside Bethlehem is not under dispute as the place where the glory of God was made visible to peasant shepherds, where the feet of angels stood in the dust of earth. The panorama of blazing effulgence sent these men to Bethlehem, obeying the mandate, "Go and see."

The Baptism of Jesus

The beginning of Jesus' public ministry was marked by His coming to the Jordan River and presenting Himself to John the Baptist for baptism. Baptism is commonplace for us today, one of the most established of all liturgical activities in the practice of the Christian faith. Twenty-first-century Christians are not surprised by the fact that Jesus was baptized, nor are we particularly excited about the ministry of John the Baptist. To a first-century Jew, however, the activity of John the Baptist was regarded as radical.

In light of the New Testament's teaching, Christians today understand baptism to be a sign of cleansing from sin. Yet the New Testament teaches that Jesus was without sin. Why would the sinless Son of God come forward and present Himself for baptism when it symbolized a cleansing from sin?

In those days John the Baptist came preaching in the wilderness of Judea, "Repent, for the kingdom of heaven is at hand." For this is he who was spoken of by the prophet Isaiah when he said, "The voice of one crying in the wilderness: Prepare the way of the Lord; make his paths straight." (Matt. 3:1–3)

The biblical narrative does not begin with the public ministry of Jesus but rather with the public ministry of John the Baptist. The voice of prophecy had been silenced in Israel for four hundred years. Between the time of Malachi and the ministry of John the Baptist, there had not been heard a single prophetic utterance. The coming of John the Baptist marked a significant departure, not only in the national history of Israel, but in what we call redemptive history. Something new was on the scene as John came fulfilling the portrait and the character of the forerunner of the Messiah.

The last prophecy found in the last paragraph of the Old Testament reads:

Remember the law of my servant Moses, the statutes and rules that I commanded him at Horeb for all Israel. "Behold I will send you Elijah the prophet before the great and awesome day of the LORD comes. And he will turn the hearts of fathers to their children and the hearts of children to their fathers, lest I come and strike the land with a decree of utter destruction." (Mal. 4:4–6)

The last Old Testament prophet, Malachi, said that before the Messiah would appear, the prophet Elijah would return. For centuries the people of Israel waited, planned, and looked for the return of Elijah. When Elijah left this world, his departure was extraordinary. He escaped the normal pangs of death, being taken up bodily into heaven in a chariot of fire. Because of his unusual departure, there was a mystique attached to this man.

The figure of John the Baptist was a strange one. He came out of the desert, the traditional meeting place between God and His people, where prophets went to commune with God and receive their marching orders from Yahweh. He was dressed in bizarre clothes, wearing a loincloth of camel hair. He ate wild locusts and honey. In short, he looked like a wild man, a misfit in society. In this, he echoed the style of Elijah.

The public response to John the Baptist was electric. As the masses poured out to see Him, the Sanhedrin sent delegates to the Jordan River to investigate. The first question they asked was, "Are you Elijah?" John replied mysteriously, "I am not . . . I am the voice of one crying in the wilderness, 'Make straight the way of the Lord.'" John said he was not Elijah. When Jesus was asked the same question about John the Baptist, He declared to His disciples, "He is the Elijah who was to come" (Matt. 11:14, NIV). His declaration was couched in enigmatic words of preface: "If you are willing to accept it." Jesus was announcing that the Old Testament prophecy of Malachi was fulfilled in the ministry of John the Baptist. There was no exact identity between John and Elijah—John was not the reincarnation of Elijah. However, he reestablished the ministry, the power, and the office of Elijah. He came in the spirit of Elijah, fulfilling the mission of Elijah.

When we pose the question, "Who is the greatest prophet in the Old Testament?" the list of candidates usually includes such prophetic titans as Isaiah, Jeremiah, Ezekiel, or Daniel. One stands above them all, laying claim to this singular honor—John the Baptist. John *was* an Old Testament prophet. His ministry is recorded in the New Testament, but his activity took place in what was still Old Testament history. Jesus declared, "All the Prophets and the Law prophesied until John" (Matt. 11:13). The word *until* in the text carries the force of "up to and including." John both closes the Old Testament line of prophets and provides a bridge, a transition to the New Testament.

Jesus declared that "among those born of women there has arisen no one greater than John the Baptist. Yet the one who is least in the kingdom of heaven is greater than he" (Matt. 11:11). How can this be? Suppose I qualify for the rank of least in the kingdom. Does that make Sproul greater than John the Baptist? Greater in what sense? More devout? More righteous? More knowledgeable? God forbid. Jesus was saying that anyone who lives on this side of the cross, this side of the resurrection, this side of the new covenant, this side of the inauguration of the kingdom of God, enjoys a far better situation, a far greater blessedness than John the Baptist. John was an eyewitness of Jesus of Nazareth and the herald of the coming kingdom of God, but he died before the kingdom was inaugurated.

John belongs to the Old Testament line of prophets, yet he differs from all of them at a crucial point. The Old Testament prophets predicted that someday the Messiah would come, a "someday" obscured by vague references to the future. John was tapped by God to be the herald, the escort who ushered in the Messiah. The "someday" became John's day. His message was not, "Repent for the kingdom is coming," but rather, "Repent, for the kingdom of heaven is at hand" (Matt. 3:2). It was at hand!

John used two important metaphors to call attention to the urgency of the hour. He said, "the axe is laid to the root of the trees" and "his winnowing fork is in his hand" (Luke 3:9, 17). John's images conjure up the vision of a woodsman who goes into the forest with his axe and begins to chop away at a huge tree. He penetrates the outer edge of the wood and sees that an enormous task remains. As his work progresses, the axe penetrates to the inner core of the tree, and the giant oak totters on one slender thread of wood. One more blow from the axe brings the tree crashing to the ground. This is the moment of breakthrough. John was declaring that the kingdom was about to come crashing through.

The image of the farmer with his "fork" in his hand was drawn from the agricultural environment of John's day. John was referring to the winnowing tool farmers used to separate the wheat from the chaff. The farmer scooped up the mixture of wheat and chaff and pitched it in the air, where the zephyrs of wind were strong enough to carry the chaff away. The farmer had gone beyond the time of preparation. He had already been to the tool shed to fetch his winnowing fork. The moment had come to pick up the fork for the task of separation. John speaks to the moment of history, the crisis moment when men will be judged whether they are for the kingdom of God or against it. The King has arrived, and His arrival brings crisis to mankind.

The baptism John initiated had many points of continuity and parallel with the later rite of baptism Jesus instituted, which became a church sacrament, but they were not precisely the same. John's baptism was designed and directed exclusively for Israel, to call the Jewish nation to readiness for the coming of their king. The roots of baptism are found in the Old Testament, where converts to Judaism from the Gentile world were subjected to a cleansing rite called proselyte baptism. For a Gentile to become a Jew, he had to do three things. He had to make a profession of faith in which he embraced the teachings of the law and the prophets; he had to be circumcised; and he had to be purified by the bath of proselyte baptism. The Gentile was considered impure and unclean. To enter into the household of Israel he had to take a bath. The radical dimension of John's ministry was that he suddenly demanded that Jews submit to baptism. The rulers of Israel did not miss the scandalous offense of John's message. John was saying: "The kingdom of God is coming and you are not ready. In the sight of God, you are as unclean and as impure as a Gentile." The humble people of the community acknowledged their need for cleansing, but the clergy were furious. John's ministry stirred up so much popular reaction that the great Jewish historian Josephus gave more space to his record of John the Baptist than to Jesus.

When Jesus appeared at the Jordan, John burst into a litany of praise, lauding Jesus as the Lamb of God. He declared that Jesus must increase while he must decrease, and that he, John, was unworthy to reach down and untie Jesus' shoes. These exalted statements fell to the ground when Jesus stepped forward and said to John, "I want you to baptize Me." John was incredulous and shrank in horror at the suggestion that he should baptize the Christ. John sought to turn the tables and have Jesus baptize him, but Christ refused.

John's understanding of theology was limited. He knew the Messiah must be the Lamb of God and he knew that the paschal lamb must be without blemish. But he was distressed that Jesus approached the river as a soiled Jewish person who needed to take a bath.

The precise words that Jesus spoke to John are important for our understanding of this event: "Let it be so now; for thus it is fitting for us to fulfill all righteousness" (Matt. 3:15). With these words, Jesus stifled a lengthy discussion about theology. In effect, He said: "Just do what I tell you, John. There is time later to seek understanding of it."

Jesus was baptized to fulfill all righteousness. This was consistent with His mission to keep every jot and tittle of the law. Jesus took on Himself every obligation that God imposed on the Jewish nation. To be the sin-bearer of the nation, it was incumbent on Him to fulfill every requirement that God demanded of Israel. Jesus was scrupulous, meticulous, indeed punctilious in His zeal for His Father's law. He was presented in the temple as an infant, He was circumcised, and He embraced the new obligation of baptism that God had imposed on the nation.

The baptism of Jesus not only carried the sign of His identification with a sinful people, it marked His consecration, His anointing for the mission the Father had given Him. His baptism sealed His doom, causing His face to be set like flint toward Jerusalem. On a later occasion, Jesus spoke to His disciples, saying, "Are you able . . . to be baptized with the baptism with which I am baptized?" (Mark 10:38). He was baptized to die. He was appointed to be the sacrificial lamb, and at His ordination the heavens opened and God spoke audibly, saying, "This is my beloved Son, with whom I am well pleased" (Matt. 3:17).

The Temptation of Christ

The New Testament records that immediately after Jesus underwent the rite of baptism, He was driven by the Holy

Spirit into the wilderness to be tempted. He had just heard the voice from heaven, saying, "This is my beloved Son, with whom I am well pleased," and the Spirit had descended on Him in the form of a dove. This same Spirit "drove" Jesus (He did not invite, request, or entice Him) into the wilderness.

How can the New Testament speak of God leading Jesus into temptation? We are explicitly told in James 1:13 that no one should say when he is tempted that he is tempted of God, for our temptations come as they arise out of our own lusts or sinful dispositions. Was Jesus an exception to this rule? The word *tempt* is used in at least two different ways in Scripture. On the one hand, there is the sense of temptation that suggests an enticing or wooing into sin. God never indulges in that. On the other hand, there is the temptation that carries the meaning of "being put to the test" or passing through a trial of moral probation. It is this meaning that describes the trial of Jesus in the wilderness.

The temptation of Christ offers a striking parallel to the probation of Adam in the Garden of Eden. We note both similarities and differences between the first Adam of Genesis and the one whom the New Testament calls the second Adam, Jesus. Both were tested not only for their own sakes but on behalf of others. Adam's trial was for the entire human race. As the federal head of mankind, Adam represented all humanity. His fall was our fall. Jesus stood for a new humanity as He faced the ardors of the new probation.

The respective locations of the tests provide a study in contrasts. Jesus' temptation took place in a desolate section of the remote hills of the Judean wilderness, a dreadful piece of real estate. The only creatures indigenous to the area were spiders, snakes, scorpions, and a few wild birds. It was rocky, barren, and hot, fit for neither man nor beast. Adam's test took place in a garden of paradise adorned with lush and glorious surroundings. Where Adam beheld a landscape of floral luxury, Jesus stared at a rock pile.

Jesus endured temptation in isolation, in what Søren Kierkegaard called the worst situation of human anxiety, existential solitude. Jesus was utterly alone. Adam was tested while enjoying the help and encouragement of a companion whom God had created for him. Adam was tested in the midst of human fellowship, indeed intimacy. However, Jesus was tested in the agony of deprivation of human communion.

Adam was tested in the midst of a feast. His locale was a gourmet's dream. He faced Satan on a full stomach and with a satiated appetite. Yet he succumbed to the temptation to indulge himself with one more morsel of food. Jesus was tested after a forty-day fast, when every fiber of His body was screaming for food. His hunger had reached a crescendo, and it was at the moment of consuming physical desire that Satan came with the temptation to break the fast.

It is the similarity, however, between the tests that is most important for us to grasp. The central issue, the point of attack, was the same. In neither case was the ultimate issue a matter of food; the issue was the question of believing God. It was not an issue of believing in God, but believing God. There was no doubt in Adam's mind that God existed; he had spent time in face-to-face communication with Him. Jesus was equally certain of God's existence. The trial centered on believing God when it counted.

The serpent, described in Genesis as the most subtle of the beasts of the field, intruded on the idyllic domain of Adam and Eve. His initial assault was not forthright but came by way of innuendo. He raised a simple question, which thinly veiled a blasphemous thought. A gossamer film of doubt was suddenly applied to the integrity of God's word. "Did God actually say, 'You shall not eat of any tree in the garden?" (Gen. 3:2).

This was a ridiculous question, so blatantly false that Eve could not miss the error of it. Like a primordial Lt. Columbo, the serpent set Eve up by appearing naive, by manipulating her to underestimate his cleverness. Eve was quick to correct the error. Of course God had made no such all-inclusive negative prohibition. Quite the contrary, God had declared that they could eat freely of all the trees of the garden, save one. The restriction was slight and trivial compared with the broad expanse of liberty granted in the garden.

The subtle hint was already made. The hidden agenda was doing its work, suggesting the idea that the French philosopher Jean-Paul Sartre formalized: If man is not totally free, if he does not enjoy autonomy, he is not truly free at all. Unless freedom is absolute, it is but an illusion, a facade hiding the reality of servitude. This was the innuendo of the serpent, a hint received not only by Eve but by all her children. If we give our assent for our children's requests fifteen times in a row, then break the streak with one *no*, the response is immediate: "You never let me do *anything*!"

Give Eve credit. She met the first wave of the serpent's assault with valor. She defended the honor of God by setting the record straight. But the serpent adroitly switched tactics, moving at once to a direct attack with a diabolical sledgehammer: "You will not surely die. . . . you will be like God" (Gen. 3:4–5). Satan was not offering a piece of fruit, but held out the promise of deification. His words were a clear and direct contradiction to what God had said.

There is tragic irony in the motto some theologians of our day have embraced. Allergic to rationality and suspicious of logic, they glory in the mixing of Christianity and existential philosophy. The motto decrees that "Contradiction is the hallmark of truth." It is said that truth is so high, so holy, that it not only transcends the power of reason, it goes against it as well. Religious truth is not only *supra*rational; it is deemed *contra*rational as well.

Apply the motto to Adam's trial. Adam, enjoying a facility of intelligence as yet unaffected by the consequences of the fall, hears the serpent's words. Immediately he recognizes that the serpent's words collide with God's. God had said that if they ate of the tree, they would die. The serpent said that if they ate, they would not die. Adam applies the canons of logic to the proposition. "If you do A, B will necessarily follow," said God. "If you do A, non B will follow," said the serpent. "Aha," muses Adam, "that violates the law of noncontradiction." Adam pursues the thought with rigorous analysis. The serpent speaks a contradiction. Contradiction is the hallmark of truth. God is truth. Q.E.D., by resistless logic, Adam's only conclusion is that the serpent is an ambassador of God. Now it is not only Adam's privilege to eat the once-forbidden fruit, but it is his moral duty. To resist the contradiction is to resist the hallmark of truth. In this mode of thinking, Adam's fall was not a fall but a great leap forward for mankind.

To call contradiction the hallmark of truth is to reach the nadir of theology. It can sink no lower. If contradiction heralds truth, we have no means to distinguish between truth and falsehood, between obedience and disobedience, between righteousness and unrighteousness, between Christ and antichrist. Biblically, contradiction is the hallmark of the lie. Truth may be mysterious, indeed even paradoxical, but never, never, never contradictory. The serpent spoke the first contradiction, and Jesus rightly declared him to be a liar from the beginning, the father of lies. Adam bought the lie. He grasped for the very throne of God, slandering the veracity of his Creator in the act.

Jesus faced the same issue in his trial. The same subtleness is employed with Satan's opening lines: "*If* you are the Son of God, command these stones to become loaves of bread" (Matt. 4:3, emphasis added). Notice Satan did not introduce his words of temptation by saying, "*Since* you are the Son of God. . . ." What were the last words to ring in the ears of Christ before He entered the wilderness? God had audibly announced from heaven, "This is my beloved Son. . . ." Such words may grow difficult to trust after enduring forty days of deprivation. Jesus was hardly enjoying the prerogatives of the Prince of Heaven. Satan's subtle attack was the same point of invasion that worked so successfully in Eden: "Did God actually say?"

Jesus foiled the subtlety by an unequivocal response: "It is written. . . ." These words were a Semitic formula for saying, "The Bible says. . . ." He rebuked Satan with a citation from Scripture: "Man shall not live by bread alone, but by every word that comes from the mouth of God" (Matt. 4:4). It was as if Jesus were saying: "Of course I am hungry. I already know I can turn stones into bread. But some things are more important than bread. I live by the Word of God. That is My life."

The Devil refused to quit. He took Jesus to the pinnacle of the temple and tested Him again: "*If* you are the Son of God, throw yourself down, for it is written, 'He will command his angels concerning you'" (Matt. 4:6, emphasis added). Satan recited Scripture, twisting it for his own purposes. The test was clear: "If God's Word is true, put it to the test—jump, and see whether the angels catch you."

Jesus answered Scripture with Scripture, reminding Satan that the Bible prohibits tempting God. Perhaps the dialogue went like this: "I perceive, Mr. Satan, that you are an astute student of the Bible. You have even committed salient parts of it to memory. But your hermeneutics are shoddy; you set

Scripture against Scripture. I know the Father has promised that He would give the angels charge over Me. I don't have to jump off pinnacles to confirm it. Right now the Father is testing Me; I am not testing Him."

Still Satan refused to surrender. He took Jesus to a high mountain and showed Him all the kingdoms of the world and said, "All these I will give you, if you will fall down and worship me" (Matt. 4:9). They were in a far country beyond the eyes of observers. No one would notice a small act of betrayal. Only a slight genuflection was necessary. Why not?

The Father had already promised Jesus all the kingdoms of the world, but the price tag was the cross. There could be no exaltation without humiliation. Satan offered an easier way. No bitter cup, no passion, no mockery. One bend of the knee and the world was Christ's.

Jesus replied, "It is written, 'You shall worship the Lord your God and him only shall you serve'" (Matt. 4:10). There could be no compromise.

Can you hear the dialogue couched in twenty-first-century terms? Satan charges: "Jesus, you are rigid and narrow-minded. Are you so pedantic about Scripture that you will choose death rather than compromise a single line of it? Don't you understand that the Law you cite is out of date? It comes from the Pentateuch, and we now know that Moses didn't even write it. It reflects the primitive beliefs of unsophisticated man, encased in primitive mythology and superstitious taboos."

"I am sorry," Jesus says. "It is Scripture, and Scripture cannot be broken."

Jesus believed God, so Satan departed from Him. Where Adam collapsed, Jesus conquered. Where Adam compromised, Jesus refused to negotiate. Where Adam's trust in God faltered, Jesus' never wavered. The second Adam triumphed for Himself and for us.

One parallel remains to be noted. At the end of Jesus' trial, angels appeared to minister to Him, precisely as the Father had promised. Adam saw an angel too. His angel was carrying a flaming sword as he stood guard at the gates of paradise. That sword banished Adam to live east of Eden.

The Passion of Christ

If any event that has transpired on this planet is too high and too holy for us to comprehend, it is the passion of Christ—His death, His atonement, and His forsakenness by the Father. We would be totally intimidated to speak of it at all were it not for the fact that God in His Word has set before us the revelation of its meaning. In this section, I want to focus on the biblical interpretation of Christ's death on the cross.

Any time we discuss a historical event, we review the facts, and sometimes we argue about what really took place, what was said, what was observed. However, once we agree on the facts (or agree to disagree), we are still left with the most important question we can ask: What is the meaning of the event?

The people who witnessed Christ stumbling toward Golgotha, who saw Him delivered to the Romans, and who watched His crucifixion, understood the significance of this event in a variety of ways. There were those present who thought that they were viewing the just execution of a criminal. Caiaphas, the high priest, said that Christ's death was expedient and that He had to die for the good of the nation. He saw the crucifixion as an act of political appeasement. A centurion who watched how Jesus died said, "Truly this was the Son of God!" (Matt. 27:54). Pontius Pilate, the two thieves who were crucified next to Jesus—everyone, it seems, had a different understanding of what the cross signified.

The cross has been a favorite theme of theological speculation for two thousand years. If we would peruse the various theological schools of thought today, we would find a multitude of competing theories as to what really happened on the cross. Some say it was the supreme illustration of sacrificial love. Others say it was the supreme act of existential courage, while still others say it was a cosmic act of redemption. The dispute goes on.

However, we have not only the record of the events in the Scriptures, primarily in the Gospels, but we also have God's interpretation of those events, primarily in the Epistles. In Galatians 3:13, Paul discusses the meaning of the cross, summarizing the entire teaching of the chapter in a single verse: "Christ redeemed us from the curse of the law by becoming a curse for us—for it is written, 'Cursed is everyone who is hanged on a tree.'"

This curse motif would have been understood clearly by a knowledgeable Jew in the ancient world, but in our day it has a foreign sound to it. To us, the very concept of "curse" smacks of something superstitious. When I hear the word *curse*, I think of Oil Can Harry in *The Perils of Pauline*, who says, "Curses, foiled again" when the hero saves the heroine from his clutches. Someone else may think of the behavior of primitive tribes who practice voodoo, in which tiny replica dolls are punctured by pins as a curse is put on an enemy. We may think of the curse of the mummy's tomb in Hollywood horror movies with Vincent Price and Bela

Lugosi. A curse in our day and age is considered something that belongs in the realm of superstition.

In biblical categories, a curse has quite a different meaning. In the Old Testament, the curse refers to the negative judgment of God. It is the antonym, the opposite, of the word *blessing*. Its roots go back to accounts of the giving of the law in the book of Deuteronomy when the covenant was established with Israel. There was no covenant without sanctions attached to it, provisions for reward for those who kept the terms of the covenant and punishment for those who violated it. God said to His people, "See, I am setting before you today a blessing and a curse—the blessing if you obey the commands of the LORD your God that I am giving you today; the curse if you disobey the commands of the LORD your God and turn from the way that I command you today by following other gods which you have not known" (Deut. 11:26–28, NIV). The curse is the judgment of God on disobedience, on violations of His holy law.

The meaning of the curse may be grasped more fully by viewing it in contrast with its opposite. The word *blessed* is often defined in Hebrew terms quite concretely. In the Old Testament, after fellowship with God was violated in Eden, people could still have a proximate relationship with God, but there was one absolute prohibition. No one was allowed to look into the face of God. That privilege, the beatific vision, was reserved for the final fulfillment of our redemption. This is the hope that we have, that someday we will be able to gaze unveiled directly into the face of God. We are still under the mandate, "man shall not see [God] and live" (Ex. 33:20). It was always the Jewish hope, however, that someday this punishment for the fall of man would be removed. The Hebrew benediction illustrates this:

> The LORD bless you and keep you;
> The LORD make his face to shine upon you and be
>   gracious to you;
> The LORD lift up his countenance upon you and give
>   you peace.
> (Num. 6:24–26)

This is an example of Hebrew parallelism. Each of the three stanzas says the same thing: May the Lord bless; may the Lord make His face shine; may the Lord lift up His countenance upon you. The Israelite understood blessedness concretely: to be blessed was to be able to behold the face of God. One could enjoy the blessing only in relative degrees: the closer one got to the ultimate face-to-face relationship, the more blessed he was. Conversely, the farther removed from that face-to-face relationship, the greater the curse. So by contrast, in the Old Testament the curse of God involved being removed from His presence altogether. The full curse precluded a glimpse, even at a distance, of the light of His countenance. It forbade even the refracted glory of one ray of the beaming light radiating from the face of Yahweh. To be cursed was to enter the place of absolute darkness outside the presence of God.

This symbolism was carried out through the history of Israel and extended to the liturgy of the Jewish people. It applied to the position of the tabernacle, the tent of meeting, which was designed to symbolize the promise that God would be in the midst of His people. God ordained that the people would pitch their tents by tribes in such a way that they were gathered around the central point of the community, where stood the tabernacle, the dwelling place of Yahweh. Only the high priest was permitted to enter into the midst of the tabernacle, the Holy of Holies, and only once a year, on the Day of Atonement. Even then, he could enter the sacred place only after lengthy ablutions and cleansing rites. God was in the midst of His people, but they could not enter the inner sanctum of the tabernacle, which symbolized His dwelling place.

On the Day of Atonement, two animals were involved

in the liturgical ceremonies, a lamb and a scapegoat. The priest sacrificed the lamb on the altar for the sins of the people. The priest also took the scapegoat and placed his hands on it, symbolizing the transfer of the sins of the nation to the back of the goat. Immediately the scapegoat was driven outside the camp into the wilderness, that barren place of remote desolation—to the outer darkness away from any proximity to the presence of God. The scapegoat received the curse. He was cut off from the land of the living, cut off from the presence of God.

In order to grasp the significance of this action as it relates to Christ's death, we must turn to the New Testament. John begins his Gospel by writing, "In the beginning was the Word, and the Word was with God, and the Word was God." The mystery of the Trinity has puzzled our minds for centuries. We know that there is a sense in which the Father and the Son are one, yet they are to be distinguished, and they exist in a unique relationship. The relationship, as John explained it, is described by the word *with*. The Word was *with* God. Literally, John was saying that Father and Son have a face-to-face relationship, precisely the type of relationship Jews were denied with the Father. The Old Testament Jew could go into the tabernacle and be "with" (Greek *sun*, meaning "with" in the sense of present in a group) God, but no one could ever be face to face with (Greek *pros*, meaning "with" in a face-to-face sense) God.

When we examine the crucifixion, it is important for us to remember that Jesus' relationship with the Father represents the ultimate in blessedness and that its absence was the essence of the curse. When we read the narrative of the passion of Jesus, certain things stand out. The Old Testament teaches us that His own people delivered Him to the Gentiles, to strangers and foreigners to the covenant. After His trial before the Jewish authorities, He was sent to the Romans for judgment. He was not executed by the Jewish method of stoning, for the circumstances of world history at that time precluded that option. When capital punishment was exercised under the Roman occupation, it had to be done by the Roman courts, so execution had to be by the Roman method of crucifixion. It is significant that Jesus was killed at the hands of the Gentiles *outside the camp*. His death took place outside the city of Jerusalem; He was taken to Golgotha. All of these activities, when woven together, indicate the reenactment of the drama of the scapegoat who received the curse.

Paul tells us that in the Deuteronomic law, the curse of God is on anyone who hangs from a tree, a curse not necessarily given to those who suffer death by stoning. Jesus hangs on a tree, fulfilling in minute detail all of the Old Testament provisions for the execution of divine judgment. The New Testament sees the death of Jesus as more than an isolated act or illustration of courage or love, though His death may illustrate those things. Rather, it is a cosmic event, an atoning death; it is a curse that is poured out on Christ for us.

The Swiss theologian Karl Barth said that the most important word in the whole New Testament is the little Greek word *huper*. The word *huper* means simply "in behalf of." The death of Jesus is in behalf of us. He takes the curse of the law for me and for you. Jesus Himself said it in many different ways: "I lay down my life for the sheep . . . No one takes it from me, but I lay it down of my own accord" (John 10:15, 18); "For even the Son of Man did not come to be served, but to serve, and to give His life as a ransom for many" (Mark 10:45, NIV). These New Testament images underscore the concept of substitution.

I once delivered a public lecture on the relationship between the old and new covenants. In the middle of my lecture, a man jumped up in the back of the room. He became outraged when I suggested that Jesus Christ's death was an atoning death, a substitutionary death on behalf of other people. He shouted from the back of the room,

"That's primitive and obscene!" After I got over my surprise and collected my thoughts, I replied, "Those are the two best descriptive words I have heard to characterize the cross."

What could be more primitive? A bloody enactment like this, with all the drama and ritual, is reminiscent of primitive taboos. It is so simple that even the most uneducated, the most simpleminded person, can understand it. God provides a way of redemption for us that is not limited to an intellectual elite but is so crass, so crude, that the primitive person can comprehend it, and, at the same time, so sublime that it brings consternation to the most brilliant theologians.

I particularly liked the second word, *obscene*. It is a most appropriate word because the cross of Christ was the most obscene event in human history. Jesus Christ became an obscenity. The moment that He was on the cross, the sin of the world was imputed to Him as it was to the scapegoat. The obscenity of the murderer, the obscenity of the prostitute, the obscenity of the kidnapper, the obscenity of the slanderer, the obscenity of all those sins, as they violate people in this world, were at one moment focused on one man. Once Christ embraced that, He became the incarnation of sin, the absolute paragon of obscenity.

There is a sense in which Christ on the cross was the most filthy and grotesque person in the history of the world. In and of Himself, He was a lamb without blemish—sinless, perfect, and majestic. But by imputation, all of the ugliness of human violence was concentrated on His person.

Once sin was concentrated on Jesus, God cursed Him. When the curse of the law was poured out on Jesus, He experienced pain that had never been suffered in the annals of history. I have heard graphic sermons about the excruciating pain of the nails in the hands, of hanging on a cross, and of the torturous dimensions of crucifixion. I am sure that they are all accurate and that it was a dreadful way to be executed, but thousands of people in world history have undergone the excruciating pain of crucifixion. Only one man has ever felt the pain of the fullness of the unmitigated curse of God on Him. When He felt it, He cried out, "My God, my God, why have you forsaken me?" (Mark 15:34, NIV). Some say He did that simply to quote Psalm 22. Others say He was disoriented by His pain and didn't understand what was happening. God certainly *did* forsake Him. That is the whole point of the atonement. Without forsakenness, there is no curse. God, at that moment in space and time, turned His back on His Son.

The intimacy of the *pros* relationship that Jesus experienced with the Father was ruptured (in His human nature). At that moment God turned out the lights. The Bible tells us that the world was encompassed with darkness, God Himself bearing witness to the trauma of the hour. Jesus was forsaken, He was cursed, and He felt it. The word *passion* means "feeling." In the midst of His forsakenness, I doubt He was even aware of the nails in His hands or the thorns in His brow. He was cut off from the Father. It was obscene, yet it was beautiful, because by it we can someday experience the fullness of the benediction of Israel. We will look unveiled into the light of the countenance of God.

The Resurrection of Jesus

The life of Jesus follows a general pattern of movement from humiliation to exaltation. The movement is not strictly linear, however, as it is interspersed with vignettes of contrast. The birth narrative contains both ignominy and majesty. His public ministry attracts praise and scorn, welcome and rejection, cries of "Hosanna!" and "Crucify Him!" Nearing the shadow of death, He exhibited the translucent breakthrough of transfiguration.

The transition from the pathos of the cross to the

grandeur of the resurrection is not abrupt. There is a rising crescendo that swells to the moment of breaking forth from the grave clothes and the shroud of the tomb. Exaltation begins with the descent from the cross immortalized in classical Christian art by the *Pieta*. With the disposition of the corpse of Jesus, the rules were broken. Under normal judicial circumstances, the body of a crucified criminal was discarded by the state, being thrown without ceremony into *gehenna*, the city garbage dump outside Jerusalem. There the body was incinerated, being subject to a pagan form of cremation, robbed of the dignity of traditional Jewish burial. The fires of *gehenna* burned incessantly as a necessary measure of public health to rid the city of its refuse. *Gehenna* served Jesus as an apt metaphor for hell, a place where the flames are never extinguished and the worm does not die.

Pilate made an exception in the case of Jesus. Perhaps he was bruised of conscience and was moved by pity to accede to the request for Jesus to be buried. Or perhaps he was moved by a mighty Providence to ensure fulfillment of the prophecy of Isaiah that Jesus would make His grave with the rich or of God's promise that He would not let His Holy One see corruption. The body of Christ was anointed with spices and wrapped in fine linen to be laid in the tomb belonging to the patrician, Joseph of Arimathea.

For three days the world was plunged into darkness. The women of Jesus' entourage wept bitterly, taking but small consolation in the permission to perform the tender act of anointing His body. The disciples had fled and were huddled together in hiding, their dreams shattered by the cry, "It is finished."

For three days God was silent. Then He screamed. With cataclysmic power, God rolled the stone away and unleashed a paroxysm of creative energy of life, infusing it once more into the still body of Christ. Jesus' heart began to beat, pumping glorified blood through glorified arteries, sending glorified power to muscles atrophied by death. The grave clothes could not bind Him as He rose to His feet and quit the crypt. In an instant, the mortal became immortal and death was swallowed up by victory. In a moment of history, Job's question was answered once and for all: "If a man die, shall he live again?" Here is the watershed moment of human history, where the misery of the race is transformed into grandeur. Here the *kerygma*, the proclamation of the early church, was born with the cry, "He is risen."

We can view this event as a symbol, a lovely tale of hope. We can reduce it to a moralism that declares, as one preacher put it, "The meaning of the resurrection is that we can face the dawn of each new day with dialectical courage." Dialectical courage is the variety invented by Frederick Nietzsche, the father of modern nihilism. Courage that is dialectical is a courage in tension. The tension is this: Life is meaningless, death is ultimate. We must be courageous, knowing that even our courage is empty of meaning. This is denial of resurrection bathed in the despair of a truncated existential hope.

However, the New Testament proclaims the resurrection as sober historical fact. The early Christians were not interested in dialectical symbols but in concrete realities. Authentic Christianity stands or falls with the space/time event of Jesus' resurrection. The term *Christian* suffers from the burden of a thousand qualifications and a myriad of diverse definitions. One dictionary defines a Christian as a person who is civilized. One can certainly be civilized without affirming the resurrection, but one cannot then be a Christian in the biblical sense. The person who claims to be a Christian while denying the resurrection speaks with a forked tongue, and we should turn away from such.

The resurrection narrative offended David Hume's test of probability quotients. It is consigned by Rudolf Bultmann to the husk of mythology that is unnecessary to the kernel of biblical truth. For Paul Van Buren, the death-of-God theologian, the resurrection is not even taught in the Bible as a real historical event. He dubs it a "discernment situation" in which the disciples suddenly came to "understand" Jesus, "seeing" Him in a new light. Van Buren's treatment violates every canon of sober literary analysis of the biblical text. That the New Testament writers were purporting to declare that a dead man came back to life is beyond serious literary dispute. One may reject the idea, but not that the idea is proclaimed.

Even Bultmann concedes the historical reality of the "Easter faith" of the early church. He reverses the biblical order, however, by arguing that it was the Easter faith that caused the proclamation of the resurrection. The Bible argues that it was the resurrection that caused the Easter faith. This subtle difference in causal nexus is the difference between faith and apostasy. The biblical writers claimed to be eyewitnesses of the risen Christ and certified the integrity of their faith with their own blood. The ancient church was willing to die for it; the modern church negotiates it, as evidenced by one major denomination's reluctance to reaffirm the bodily resurrection on the grounds that it is divisive. Faith in the resurrection of Christ is indeed divisive, as it divided the Christians from the gladiators and prompted the hostile Nero to illumine his garden with human torches.

The resurrection of Jesus is radical in the original sense of the word. It touches the *radix*, the "root" of the Christian faith. Without it, Christianity becomes just another religion designed to titillate our moral senses with platitudes of human wisdom.

The apostle Paul spelled out the clear and irrefutable consequences of a "resurrectionless" Christianity. If Christ is not raised, he reasoned, we are left with the following list of conclusions (1 Cor. 15:13–19):

1. Our preaching is futile.
2. Our faith is in vain.
3. We have misrepresented God.
4. We are still in our sins.
5. Our loved ones who have died have perished.
6. We are of all men most to be pitied.

These six consequences sharply reveal the inner connection of the resurrection to the substance of Christianity. The resurrection of Jesus is the *sine qua non* of the Christian faith. Take away the resurrection and you take away Christianity.

The biblical writers do not base their claim of resurrection on its internal consistency to the whole of faith, however. It is not simply a logical deduction drawn from other doctrines of faith. It is not that we must affirm the resurrection because the alternatives to it are grim. Resurrection is not affirmed because life would be hopeless or intolerable without it. The claim is based not on speculation but on empirical data. They saw the risen Christ. They spoke with Him and ate with Him. Neither His death nor His resurrection happened in a corner like Joseph Smith's alleged reception of special revelation. The death of Jesus was a public spectacle and a matter of public record. The resurrected Christ was seen by more than five hundred people at one time. The Bible presents history on this matter.

The strongest objection raised against the biblical account of Jesus' resurrection is the same objection raised against other biblical miracles, namely, that such an event is impossible. It is ironic that the New Testament approaches the question of Christ's resurrection from exactly the opposite direction. In Peter's speech on Pentecost, he declared: "God raised him up, loosing the pangs of death, because it was not possible for him to be held by it" (Acts 2:24).

To set forth the principle stated here, I must indulge myself with the use of a double negative. It was impossible for Christ *not* to have been raised. For death to have held Christ would have required the supreme and unthinkable violation of the laws of death. It is viewed by modern man as an inexorable law of nature that what dies stays dead. However, that is a law of fallen nature. In the Judeo-Christian view of nature, death entered the world as a judgment on sin. The Creator decreed that sin was a capital offense: "In the day that you eat of it you shall surely die" (Gen. 2:17) was the original warning. God granted an extension of life beyond the day of sin, but not indefinitely. The original sanction was not completely rescinded. Mother Nature became the paramount executioner. Adam was created with both the possibility of death (*posse mori*) and the possibility of avoiding it (*posse non mori*). By his transgression, he forfeited the possibility of avoidance of death and incurred, as judgment, the impossibility of not dying (*non posse non mori*).

Jesus was not Adam. He was the second Adam. He was free from sin, both original and actual. Death had no legitimate claim on Him. He was punished for the sin imputed to Him, but once the price was paid and the imputation was lifted from His back, death lost its power. In death, an atonement was made; in resurrection, the perfect sinlessness of Jesus was vindicated. He was, as the Scriptures assert, raised for our justification as well as His own vindication.

Hume's probability quotients discard the resurrection because it was a unique event. He was right on one count. It was a unique event. Though Scripture relates other resurrection accounts, such as the raising of Lazarus, they were all in a different category. Lazarus died again. The uniqueness of Jesus' resurrection was tied to another aspect of His uniqueness. It was tied to His sinlessness, a dimension of the person of Jesus that would be even more unique if uniqueness were capable of degrees.

For God to allow Jesus to be bound forever by death would have been for God to violate His own righteous character. It would have been an injustice, an act that is supremely impossible for God to commit. The surprise is not that Jesus rose, but that He stayed in the tomb as long as He did. Perhaps it was God's condescension to human weakness of unbelief that inclined Him to keep Christ captive, to ensure that there would be no doubt He was dead and that the resurrection would not be mistaken for a resuscitation.

The resurrection sets Jesus apart from every other central figure of world religions. Buddha is dead. Mohammed is dead. Confucius is dead. None of these were sinless. None offered atonement. None were vindicated by resurrection.

If we stagger with unbelief before the fact of resurrection, we would do well to consider the plight of the two walking to Emmaus that weekend. Luke records the event for us (Luke 24:13–35.). As the two men were walking away from Jerusalem, Jesus joined them incognito. They presumed to inform Jesus about the events of the crucifixion and showed obvious impatience with His apparent ignorance of the matters. When they related the report of the women concerning the resurrection, Christ rebuked them:

> "O foolish ones, and slow of heart to believe all that the prophets have spoken! Was it not necessary that the Christ should suffer these things and enter into his glory?" And beginning with Moses and all the Prophets, he interpreted to them in all the Scriptures the things concerning himself.

When the two had their eyes opened and they recognized Jesus that night, they said to each other, "Did not our hearts burn within us while he talked to us on the road, while he opened to us the Scriptures?"

A Christian is not a skeptic. A Christian is a person with a burning heart, a heart set aflame with certainty of the resurrection.

The Ascension of Christ

My graduate work in theology in Amsterdam provoked a crisis in my Christian life. The crisis was triggered by a technical study of the doctrine of the ascension. Like most Protestants, I had neglected this theme, considering it an unscientific postscript to the life of Christ, not worthy of special commemoration like Christmas and Easter. The event is described only twice in the New Testament. I am now convinced that no single event in the life of Jesus is more important than the ascension, not even the crucifixion or the resurrection. It is dangerous business to assign relative values to the episodes of Christ's life and ministry, but if we underestimate the significance of the ascension, we sail in perilous waters.

What could be more important than the cross? Without it we have no atonement, no redemption. Paul resolved to preach Christ and Him crucified. Yet without the resurrection, we would be left with a dead Savior. Crucifixion and resurrection go together, each borrowing some of its value from the other. However, the story does not end with the empty tomb. To write *finis* there is to miss a climactic moment of redemptive history, a moment toward which both Old and New Testaments move with inexorable determination. The ascension is the apex of Christ's exaltation, the acme of redemptive history to this point. It is the pregnant moment of Christ's coronation as King. Without it, the resurrection ends in disappointment and Pentecost would not be possible.

My crisis experience in Holland was provoked by a study of one obscure statement from the lips of Christ. On an occasion when Jesus told His disciples of His impending death, He said, "Where I am going you cannot follow me now" (John 13:36), and, "Yet a little while and the world will see me no more" (John 14:19). Jesus continued His discourse by explaining, "It is to your advantage that I go away" (John 16:7). Here Jesus was making a value judgment about His departure. The thrust of His comment was to suggest that His absence was better for His disciples than His presence. This must have strained the understanding of His friends to the uttermost limits. *Prima facia,* it is unthinkable that under any circumstances people could benefit more from the absence of Jesus than from His presence, save for those unfortunate ones who face His judgment and would welcome a respite from Him. The Christian longs for the abiding presence of Christ. The contemporary Christian grows wistful imagining what it must have been like to have seen and known the incarnate Christ when He walked the earth. Millions travel annually to Palestine just to see where He lived and ministered. Surely the church has either failed to grasp the import of Jesus' words or has simply been unable to believe them. We live as if there had been no ascension.

The disciples were slow in grasping the expediency of Jesus' departure. They resisted His determination to go to Jerusalem and took umbrage at His announcements of His coming death. Between the resurrection and the ascension, new light dawned on them as they began to undergo a remarkable change of attitude. The culmination in the change was evidenced by their immediate reaction to Jesus' visible elevation into heaven. They did not exhibit the normal human reaction to such a departure. The record says the disciples "returned to Jerusalem *with great joy*" (Luke 24:52, emphasis added).

Parting may be sweet sorrow, but the normal measure of sweetness is unable to turn sorrow into rejoicing. When men ship out for war or sailors go to sea, there are more tears than smiles on the faces of loved ones left behind. I remember tugging at my father's duffle bag when he started for the troop train at the end of a furlough during World War II. There was no joy in it. I remember the end of Christmas vacation and the ritual that took place at the Greyhound bus terminal during my college days, when I would put my fiancée on a bus to return to school after we had enjoyed a brief interlude together. I did not return to my school rejoicing.

To be sure, the disciples had to be prodded by an angel to leave the spot where Christ departed on the Mount of Olives. They stood there transfixed, savoring the vision of the glory cloud enveloping Jesus. They were rooted to the spot, spellbound by the vista of majesty surrounding them. Their reverie was broken by the words of the angel: "Men of Galilee, why do you stand looking into heaven? This Jesus, who was taken up from you into heaven, will come in the same way as you saw him go into heaven" (Acts 1:11).

They returned to Jerusalem. They must have been giddy: laughing, skipping, and singing the whole way. They recalled the words of Jesus in the upper room of the promise of another Comforter who would come. They were glad in heart because they finally understood where Jesus was going and why He was going there.

Earlier, Christ had said, "No one has ascended into heaven but he who descended from heaven" (John 3:13). He was speaking of Himself. These words placed the ascension squarely in the category of the unique event. In His ascension, Jesus displayed again that He was in a class by

Himself. No one before or since has "ascended" to heaven. The prerequisite for ascension was a prior descent. As the only-begotten incarnate Christ, Jesus was singularly qualified for this event. Others had gone to heaven. Enoch was "translated" and Elijah was "taken up." One could "ascend" a ladder (Jesus had told Nathanael that he would see angels ascending and descending on the Son of Man, and Jacob beheld a ladder in his midnight dream at Bethel) or one could "ascend" to Jerusalem, moving to a higher elevation from sea level. The term could be used figuratively to refer to the elevation of a king to his royal office. But no one ever had "ascended to heaven" in the sense in which Jesus was speaking.

The ascension of Jesus was the supreme political event of world history. He ascended not so much to a place as to an office. He departed from the arena of humiliation and suffering to enter into His glory. In one moment, He leapfrogged from the status of despised Galilean teacher to the cosmic King of the universe, jumping over the heads of Pilate, Herod, and all the other rulers of the earth. The ascension catapulted Jesus to the right hand of God, where He was enthroned as King of kings and Lord of lords. Here the political "expediency" of His departure stands out in bold relief.

The implications of this event for the church are

staggering. It means that though we suffer persecution and the scorn of hostile power structures—though we groan under the demeaning status of an unwelcome minority—our candidate sits in the seat of sovereign authority. The kingdom of God is not an unrealized dream or religious fantasy. The investiture of our King is a *fait accompli*. His reign is neither mythical nor illusory. It corresponds to a real state of affairs. At this very moment, the Lord God omnipotent reigns with His Son at His right hand, in the seat of imperial authority. To be sure, the kingdom is yet to be consummated—that is future. However, it has been inaugurated. That is past. He reigns in power, possessing all authority in heaven and earth. That is present. His kingdom is invisible but no less real. It is left to His church to make His invisible kingship visible.

Christ's ascension to the right hand of God is inseparably linked to the coming of Pentecost. In a certain sense, Jesus lacked the authority to dispatch the Spirit prior to His ascension. One of the first acts of authority He exercised after His enthronement was to endow His church with power from on high. His disciples were given a great commission, a mandate to penetrate the whole world bearing witness to the kingdom. These were and are to be the authentic witnesses of Yahweh. However, no border was to be crossed or mission undertaken until first the Spirit came down. The disciples returned to Jerusalem rejoicing for the purpose of their wait; they were waiting for Pentecost. When the new King of the cosmos sent the Holy Spirit, the power of the kingdom was unleashed on the world.

Christ's elevation was not only political, it was also sacerdotal. He assumed not only the scepter of the King but the garments of the High Priest as well. In His ascension, Jesus entered the sanctuary as well as the palace. Not only does Jesus sit at the right hand of God, He kneels. He has entered the *sanctus sanctorum*, the Holy of Holies, to make daily intercession for His people. We are a people whose King prays for us by name.

Do you wonder, then, at the disciples' joy? Once they understood where Jesus was going and why He was going there, the only appropriate response was celebration. They danced back to Jerusalem. His physical presence was gone, but His spiritual and political presence was enhanced. His words console his "absent" bride: "And behold, I am with you always, to the end of the age" (Matt. 28:20).

About the Author

Dr. R. C. Sproul is the founder and chairman of Ligonier Ministries, an international multimedia ministry based in Lake Mary, Florida. He also serves as senior minister of preaching and teaching at Saint Andrew's in Sanford, Florida, and his teaching can be heard on the daily radio program *Renewing Your Mind*.

During his distinguished academic career, Dr. Sproul helped train men for the ministry as a professor at several leading theological seminaries.

He is the author of more than sixty books, including *The Holiness of God*, *Chosen by God*, *The Invisible Hand*, *Faith Alone*, *A Taste of Heaven*, *Truths We Confess*, *The Truth of the Cross*, and *The Prayer of the Lord*. He also served as general editor of *The Reformation Study Bible* and has written several children's books, including *The Prince's Poison Cup*.

Dr. Sproul and his wife, Vesta, make their home in Longwood, Florida.